Ireland's Call

Ireland's Call

Six Nations Success:
Irish Sporting Legends

Paul O'Flynn

Gill Books

Gill Books
Hume Avenue
Park West
Dublin 12
www.gillbooks.ie

Gill Books is an imprint of M.H. Gill & Co.

First published in 2024. This paperback edition published 2026.

978 18045 8545 0

Print origination by Typo•glyphix
Edited by Natasha Mac a'Bháird
Proofread by Kathy Woolley
Printed and Bound in the UK using 100% Renewable Electricity at CPI
Group (UK) Ltd.
This book is typeset in 12pt on 18pt, Tahoma.

For permission to reproduce artwork, the author and publisher gratefully
acknowledge the following: © Adobe Stock/longquattro

The paper used in this book comes from the wood pulp of sustainably
managed forests.

This book has been produced in accordance with guidelines provided by
Dyslexia Ireland.

*To the best of our knowledge, this book complies in full with the
requirements of the General Product Safety Regulation (GPSR). For
further information and help with any safety queries, please contact us
at productsafety@gill.ie.*

A CIP catalogue record for this book is available from the British Library.

5 4 3 2 1

Author's Note

This book tells the inside story of Ireland's epic Six Nations win. It would be impossible for me to go back and listen in to all the conversations between the players over the years, so I have had to imagine them. I also haven't actually been in the dressing rooms or inside the players heads, because that would just be weird! However, all of the scores and matches are real and all the achievements of the players mentioned in the book are factual. This Ireland team really is one of the best to ever play the game of rugby!

About the Author

Paul O'Flynn is an RTÉ News and Sport presenter and journalist. A graduate of DCU with a BA in Journalism and an MA in International Relations, he is also currently an associate lecturer at his alma mater. He is a keen sportsperson and amateur swimmer, and in 2018 he was the winner of the Liffey Swim. This is his fourth book in the Irish Sporting Legends series.

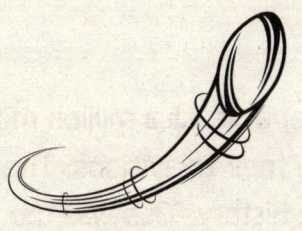

Chapter 1

Heartbreak

Paris didn't know what had hit it. The capital of France, home of the Eiffel Tower, the Arc de Triomphe and the Mona Lisa, a city of 11 million people – and today it had been painted green. Tens of thousands of Irish fans had arrived by plane, train and boat. Now they took over the streets, cafes and bars, singing, dancing and waving their green, white and orange flags. They had tickets to the hottest match of the Rugby World Cup. Ireland v the All Blacks.

Back home, at least a million more fans were glued to their televisions. They were all hoping to see history. This was the biggest game ever in Irish rugby: the World Cup quarter-final at the Stade de France. Everything was on the line.

Ireland were the number-one-ranked team in the world and up to now they'd been having the perfect World Cup. Everything had gone to plan, right from their very first match against Romania. It had been an exhibition. Captain Johnny Sexton, Bundee Aki, Peter O'Mahony and Tadhg Beirne all scored two tries each in a thumping 82-8 win.

It was a similar story in the next match against Tonga. Bundee Aki scored two more tries, while Johnny Sexton added another to become Ireland's all-time leading points scorer in all competitions. Ireland were flying. But tougher tests lay ahead.

The most difficult match of the pool stage was against the defending World Champions, South Africa. It promised to be epic and that's exactly how it played out. South Africa were a huge, strong team. They were so powerful they were known as 'the bomb squad'. It was a thrilling game from the first whistle. One of the best anyone had ever seen. South Africa used their strength and speed. But Ireland were able for everything they threw at them. Flying winger Mack Hansen scored a first-half try to put Ireland in front.

It was all going to plan. Suddenly, South Africa struck back in an end-to-end bruising battle. The game went by in a flash. Both teams gave it everything. Ireland had their noses in front as the clock ticked down, but they were hanging on. It was so close!

South Africa pushed and pushed for a late score to win the match. But in the end, Ireland's defence held firm. Ireland won by 13 points to 8. The fans went wild and the players celebrated long into the night. It was a huge victory. They had just beaten the reigning world champions. But they felt they were only getting started.

Ireland's next match was against Scotland. Once more they put in a perfect performance to book their place in the quarter-finals. The tries flowed, as a whole host of players crossed over the line. Full-back Hugo Keenan scored twice, along with James Lowe, Iain Henderson, Dan Sheehan and Garry Ringrose. The game finished 36-14 to Ireland. Another big win. Now everybody was saying Ireland were the clear favourites to win the World Cup. But first, they faced a tricky test against the mighty All Blacks.

In the knockout stages, the tournament started for real. Everything was on the line in this do-or-die clash in Paris. Win and Ireland were into the semi-finals of the World Cup for the first time ever. Lose and they were going home.

Captain Johnny Sexton looked around the stadium as he was warming up. He knew this could be his last ever match in a green shirt. He wanted to take in every minute of it.

The national anthems were bellowed out across the Stade de France. Each and every player on the Irish team trembled with emotion as they sang 'Ireland's Call' together.

'Come the day and come the hour ... Come the power and the glory ...'

Then it was time for action.

The referee blew his whistle. But Ireland were caught cold. Before they knew it, they were 6-0 down. Soon, it got even worse. Leicester Fainga'anuku broke clear for the first try of the match for the All Blacks. Ireland were 13-0 behind.

Johnny and his teammates couldn't believe it.

'Don't drop your heads,' roared Johnny. 'There's still plenty of time.'

He knew this team had come through too much together to give up now. They started to claw their way back into the game. Their confidence grew. Suddenly, the indestructible Bundee Aki found some space.

Bundee Aki steps ... Bundee Aki's in! Tryyyyy!

It was a super try for Ireland. The fans roared with delight. It was game on now.

But the All Blacks came again. This time Ardie Savea leapt into the corner for another try.

Once more, Ireland found another gear. They swung again with a punch of their own. Jamison Gibson-Park did the damage and scored!

It was breathless. The ball was moving from one end of the field to the other. The players were so tired and it was only half-time. Even the fans watching could hardly keep up. It was 18-17 to the All Blacks. It was one of the most exciting games ever played at a World Cup.

***

'Keep your heads!' said Ireland's coach Andy Farrell in the dressing room. 'You've done the hard part. You've recovered from the bad start. Just play your game and the scores will come.'

'Come on, boys!' screamed James Lowe, as they made their way back out onto the pitch.

The drama kept on coming. First, All Black winger Will Jordan showed his speed to slip past the Irish defence. But again, Ireland refused to accept defeat.

Heartbreak

Here comes the green machine ... It's a penalty try!

Nobody could believe how close this game was. There was just one point in it now. Suddenly, New Zealand got a penalty and slotted it over. They were four points in front with just minutes left to play. Ireland had to score a try or they would be out of the World Cup.

Time after time the Irish players crashed into the All Black defence. It was like waves crashing against the shore. They just couldn't find the space. They attacked 35 times in a row in the dying stages of the match. The clock was against them and finally, agonisingly close to the line, they lost the ball. The referee blew the full-time whistle.

The All Black players raised their hands in victory. One by one Ireland's players fell to the ground in disbelief. Their World Cup dream was over. Captain Johnny Sexton's perfect send-off was not to be. Their hopes had been crushed.

Many fans were in tears inside the stadium. They clapped and cheered the players even though they had lost. They had given it everything. But in sport, sometimes that just isn't enough. Winger Keith Earls waved to the fans too. He was also saying goodbye after a lifetime of success.

It was the end of an era. The end of Ireland's World Cup campaign. The end of Johnny Sexton's glorious career in green. The end of a shared dream between this band of brothers who had worked so hard together to make it come true.

But one man in the stadium didn't see it as the end. Coach Andy Farrell stood in the centre of the pitch and consoled the players. He was as disappointed as any of them. He really had believed this was Ireland's time. But in his mind, he was already planning for the future. He was a born winner and he knew that there was only one thing to do when you lose. Go again. Try again. Fail again. Fail better. He knew there would be brighter days ahead and was already making plans for next season.

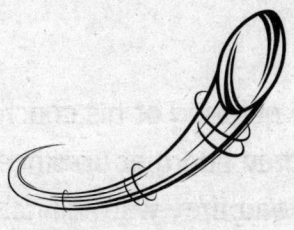

Chapter 2

Rebuild

The players took a well-earned break
after the World Cup. It was a chance for
them to rest their tired bodies. And, more
importantly, to restore their tired minds.
They had worked so hard together on their
World Cup dream, the disappointment was
going to take a long time to get over. But
Andy Farrell didn't take much time off. He
was soon back to work, planning for the new
Six Nations season.

He called a meeting of his coaches. It was the first time they had met up since the World Cup in France and they were all itching to get going again. They had so much experience in the game, and they all had ideas for how to make the Ireland team even better.

Forwards coach Paul O'Connell was one of the best players ever to play for Ireland and Munster. He was a master of the lineout and when he spoke, the players listened to his every word. Assistant coach Mike Catt had a stellar career for England and played in two World Cup finals. Simon Easterby was another legend who played 65 times for Ireland. He oversaw the defence now and he hated nothing more than when the opposition scored a try. And John Fogarty was the scrum coach. He won the European Champions Cup playing with Leinster and was an expert in the dark arts of the scrum.

'I want you all to be open and honest,' said Andy Farrell, as they sat together to review the World Cup. He was a tall, tough man with jet-black hair and a thick beard who had won everything as a player in England. Now he had taken Irish rugby to new heights. He commanded the respect of everyone in the game.

'That's the only way we can understand what we did right and what we got wrong,' he continued. 'That's how we will get better together.'

The coaches chatted for a long time. They agreed they didn't need to change much. They hadn't become the number one team in the world by doing things badly. They seemed to be getting most things right.

Some fans and media said it was time for a big change. It was four years until the next World Cup. A chance perhaps to bring through a young team and let them grow together. But Andy didn't agree with this. His old coach at Wigan, Graham Lowe, always said it was better to change a team slowly rather than quickly. They had a lot of success together. Andy agreed it was better to bring through one or two young players every year.

But he and his coaches still had some big decisions to make. The retirement of Johnny Sexton left a huge hole in the Irish squad. It was going to take two men to replace him. One as the new captain. And another as the new out-half, the team's playmaker and kicker in the famous number 10 jersey.

As they drank tea and ate biscuits, they discussed all the players in contention. It was one of Andy's favourite things about not being a player anymore. He could eat as many biscuits as he wanted!

For Andy, the captaincy was the most important. A captain needs certain skills. The most important is leadership. Some players are quiet and like to lead by example. They do all the right things in training and on the pitch and make sure that other players follow their lead. Others, like Johnny, have big personalities. They lead by telling other players what to do and giving them a piece of their mind when they don't.

There were several players in the running to be the new captain. One of the favourites was

Rebuild

Peter O'Mahony. He had captained Munster for ten years and was a central player in the glory years of Irish rugby. But like Johnny and his Munster teammate Keith Earls, he was coming to the end of his career. Nobody knew yet if he was going to continue to play for Ireland. He had decided to step away from captaining Munster and there was a big question mark over whether he thought his time in the green jersey was over too.

Then there was James Ryan, the tall and athletic Leinster lock-forward who had filled in as captain before. He was from a family of politicians, so leadership was in his blood. Garry Ringrose, the Leinster co-captain, was also being considered. Others felt it was time to give the captain's armband to the next generation of younger players, like hooker Dan Sheehan or number 8, Caelan Doris.

'It's a great decision to have to make,' said Andy. 'We're spoiled for choice!'

Next, and maybe just as importantly, was picking Johnny Sexton's replacement as

out-half. The man temporarily in possession
of the jersey was Jack Crowley, the young
Munster out-half who had served as back-up
number 10 at the World Cup. But once again,
Andy and his coaches had plenty of options.
Ross Byrne, the Leinster out-half, had played
many times for Ireland before injury ruined
his World Cup chances. He was a superb
kicker who never let anyone down. Ross's
brother, Harry, was also in the mix. He was a
skilful player, who played rather like Johnny
Sexton. Ciarán Frawley was another with all
the skills to step up. Sam Prendergast was
also making waves at Leinster. Was he too
young to take the big step up?

The coaches talked for hours, but in the
end, it was a decision only Andy could make.
'I'm going to sleep on it,' he told the others.
He needed a bit more time to make up his
mind.

'Before we go, I've something else to tell
you,' said Andy. 'I wanted you to hear it from
me first.'

Rebuild

The other coaches looked surprised.

'I've been given the nod to take over the Lions,' he said. 'But not a word to anyone. It's still a secret!'

'Good man, Andy!' said Simon Easterby, grinning.

'Congrats, big man!' said Paul O'Connell, as he slapped Andy on the back.

'Cheers, Paulie,' replied Andy, smiling.

It was a huge honour. Andy Farrell had been chosen as head coach for the British and Irish Lions tour to Australia in 2025.

The Lions brings together the best players in Ireland, England, Scotland and Wales to play as one team. It only happens once every four years and it's the highest honour in rugby to play in a Lions test match.

As one of the best coaches in the world, Andy had long been in the running for the job. Now it was official.

But this presented a headache for Ireland. Andy had to take on the job full-time. So it was agreed he would take a break from coaching the Irish team at the end of the season. He would work with the Lions for a year before returning to Ireland again. That meant the upcoming Six Nations was his last chance to win a trophy with Ireland for a while. He really didn't want the opportunity to pass him by. He had two big decisions to make. It was time he made up his mind.

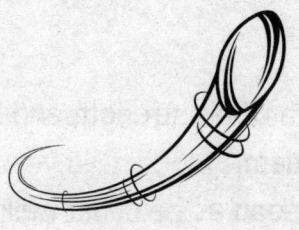

Chapter 3

Made in Cork

Peter O'Mahony was born to captain Ireland.
He didn't know it himself. But all the signs were
there from the very first days of his life. His
dad, John, was a famous player on the club
scene in Cork. He spent so much of his life
playing, working and helping at the famous
Cork Con club that he was known everywhere
as 'Con John'. Peter's mother, Caroline, was a
strong sportswoman herself. She was from a
well-known family of rowers in Cork, and Peter

inherited much of his strength and love of fitness from them.

Almost as soon as he could walk, Peter spent most of his time at the rugby club. Everywhere his father went, Peter was sure to follow. When his dad played a match, Peter looked on from the sideline. The substitutes took turns babysitting him, as the wide-eyed youngster took everything in.

'Come on, Dad!' he would roar proudly, as he watched his dad launch into another fierce tackle.

***

At the age of five, Peter was allowed to join the club himself. He was so excited. Cork Con was one of the most successful clubs in Ireland. Legendary players like Donal Lenihan, Ronan O'Gara, Peter Stringer and Donncha O'Callaghan had all passed through before him. It was in his blood. Peter had spent so long preparing for this moment, practising lineouts and scrums in the garden with his dad. He couldn't believe the day had come.

It was a wet and windy Saturday morning. Peter was all kitted out in club gear, with his gumshield tightly in place and his knees already caked in mud. Just a few minutes into the first training session, the coach took a good look at him.

'What's the story with that lad?' he asked one of the parents on the sideline. 'This is for beginners. Are you sure he's only five?'

The man laughed. 'That's Con John's son, Peter,' he said. 'He's been hanging around here since he was born!'

'Send him up to the under-8s,' barked the coach. 'He's nearly a man already!' he said, joking.

That was the start of a glorious career on the pitch for the great Peter O'Mahony. His younger brothers Mark and Cian came along too. And they all spent many years together at the club. Peter was a great player when he was a boy. He usually played at out-half, number 10, showing all his skills and running the game. He loved to get stuck in and he was a natural leader too. By the age of 12, he was chosen to captain the team.

Around the same time, he started secondary school and began a new life at Pres Cork. It was a well-known school where rugby was a religion. But even the teachers there hadn't seen anyone like Peter before. He had rugby on the brain.

One day, his English teacher asked the boys to write a short story using a word beginning with every letter of the alphabet. It didn't take Peter long to get going. A for 'Attack', B for 'Breakdown', C for 'Conversion', D for 'Defence' ... On and on he went ... W for 'Winger', X for 'Extra time', Y for 'Yellow card' ... Peter's stories were all about rugby. He thought he was a genius. The teacher wasn't quite so impressed.

Hopefully some day you will grow up to play for Munster. And maybe even Ireland, she wrote at the bottom of his homework sheet. Little did she know.

His most treasured possession was a photo

of himself with the brilliant All Blacks winger Jonah Lomu. He hung it on his bedroom wall with pride.

In the early days at secondary school, Peter changed his position on the rugby pitch. He was getting bigger and stronger and loved getting more and more involved in tackling and blocking other players. His coaches felt his skills would be better used in the forward pack, and he happily agreed. He began his new life as a second row and would later find his best position as a flanker.

Typically, Peter threw himself headfirst into new tasks. At break-time in school, he organised lineouts in the yard. Calling the shots and perfecting his jumps. So it was no surprise that within a few years, Peter and his teammates powered their way to success in the Munster Schools Senior Cup. They beat local rivals Christians 13-3 in the final at Musgrave Park. Peter's great friend and future Munster and Ireland teammate Simon Zebo scored the winning try.

O'Donoghue ... A loose kick downfield into the arms of Simon Zebo ... Zebo shows his pace ... Cuts inside past one ... two ... three defenders. He's on his way to the try line ... Oh my goodness! He's going all the way!

Tryyyyy!

Simon Zebo's virtuoso try has won it for Pres!

It was Peter's first taste of major silverware, and it made him want more. As he grew from a boy into a man, he moved up to the senior team at Cork Con and was soon on the fast track to superstardom. He was quickly called up to Munster and then Ireland, captaining the under-18s and the under-20s. Things were happening fast. Another year later, he broke into the senior Munster team, rubbing shoulders with legends like Anthony Foley, Paul O'Connell and Ronan O'Gara. Before long, he was captaining the side, just like every other team he ever played for. By his mid-20s, he was already considered a Munster legend himself. It was some rise to the top.

Alongside his success at Munster, Peter became a rock at the heart of the Irish team. A nailed-on starter in the number 6 shirt. He was a warrior that every player wanted on their team. In the green of Ireland, he was even more successful than in the red of Munster. In ten glorious years, he won four Six Nations titles, two Grand Slams and three Triple Crowns. He was one of the most decorated players in the history of the game.

But now he was coming to the end, at the age of 34. The World Cup in France had broken his heart. Peter really believed Ireland were going to win it. Johnny Sexton and Keith Earls had decided to retire. Peter had soldiered with them for years. Maybe it was time for him to finish up too, he thought. He had decided to step down as Munster captain before the World Cup. Many felt this was a sign that he was ready to walk away from the game he had loved since he was a boy.

When he came home from France, he took a while to rest and recover. He enjoyed having

more time to spend with his wife Jessica
and his three young children, Indie, Theo
and Ralph. It also meant he could pay more
attention to his garden. His favourite place!
Peter loved working his lawn, cutting the grass
and weeding to get it just right. Gardening was
his ultimate way to unwind.

One day when he was pushing the
lawnmower, trying to get every blade of grass
cut to perfection, his phone rang suddenly. It
was Andy Farrell.

'Hello!' shouted Peter over the din of the
lawnmower. 'Give me a sec!'

He turned off the lawnmower and the blade
spun slowly to a stop.

'That's better. Howya, Andy!' said Peter, as
he wiped the sweat from his forehead.

'Listen, Pete,' said Andy. 'I know the World
Cup is just over. I don't know what you're
thinking. But the other coaches and I have
been chatting and plotting a way forward.'

Peter raised an eyebrow. He knew where
this was going.

'Anyway,' continued Andy. 'I think there's loads more in this team. I think we've a lot more to achieve together. And I want you to be the captain. I want you to bring this next generation forward.'

Peter felt a shiver down his spine. It was everything he had ever dreamed of. He had captained every team he had ever played with. Cork Con, his school Pres, the Ireland under-18s and under-20s, Munster and the British and Irish Lions. Now came the ultimate prize.

'Of course,' he said quickly, cutting Andy off. 'I'd be honoured. And I won't let you down.'

'Well, that settles that,' said Andy. 'Looking forward to working with you!'

Peter fired up the lawnmower again and a smile came to his face.

'Let's go!' he thought to himself.

From his first footsteps in Cork Con Rugby Club all those years ago, he had just become the captain of Ireland. He'd known all along that he was born for this moment.

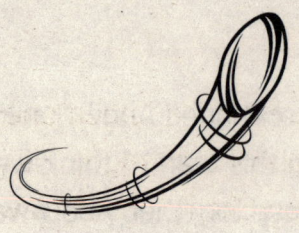

Chapter 4

Big Boots to Fill

Sorting out the captaincy meant one less headache for Andy Farrell. He was delighted Peter O'Mahony had agreed to stay on to lead the team. He knew Peter was the best man for the job. But now Andy had to answer another big question. Who would fill Johnny Sexton's boots at out-half?

Once again, the answer lay in Munster. And in Cork. More specifically, in the town of Bandon.

Big Boots to Fill

Johnny Sexton had been one of the all-time greats of Irish rugby. He had won four European Champions Cups with Leinster and four Six Nations with Ireland, including two Grand Slams. He was Ireland's record points scorer and was a former World Player of the Year. He had done it all. He was almost impossible to replace. But Andy Farrell was confident he had found the right man.

Bandon in West Cork isn't exactly the first place you would look to find Ireland's next rugby superstar. But that's where Jack Crowley took his first steps on the rugby field. His family were rugby mad. His dad Fachtna played for Bandon for years, along with his uncles and a gang of cousins. Jack's older brothers, Jerry and Billy, and his sister Tessa all played rugby for the club, so it was no surprise that Jack followed in their footsteps when the time came. In fact, their family was so rugby mad that their house was easy to spot. They lived in Innishannon, just a short trip outside Bandon. Everyone in the area knew the Crowleys' home as it had rugby posts in the garden.

It was clear for all to see that Jack had an exceptional talent. He always seemed to have more time on the ball than anyone else. He had great skills. And he was brave. He had everything needed to make it to the top. Most importantly, he worked incredibly hard and always listened to his coaches to help him get even better.

By the age of 12, he was already being talked about as a player who could make it all the way to the top. He loved watching Munster and Ireland matches with his family. His favourite player at the time was Peter O'Mahony. One year, at the end of the season, the club had a barbecue for all the players. The children were told that special guests had been invited to hand out medals and trophies. Jack and his teammates were thrilled. Who would the special guests be?

They lined up along the pitch, as a car pulled up. Jack could barely contain his excitement as he craned his neck to see who it was. There was a loud gasp when not one, but two Munster players stepped out of the car. It was Peter O'Mahony and Simon Zebo.

All the young players ran to the car to surround them, giving high fives and asking for autographs. Eventually, Jack's turn came. He got a photo taken with his two heroes.

'Say cheese!' said Jack's dad, as he took the photo. Peter O'Mahony, Simon Zebo and 12-year-old Jack Crowley all smiled for the camera. Little did they know then that 10 years later the three of them would be teammates.

Away from rugby, Jack loved playing golf or relaxing with his family at home. But his favourite thing to do was play with his pet labrador puppies. He loved dogs and his family had a special job. They helped raise guide dog puppies for the blind.

Labradors are exceptional at helping visually impaired people, making sure they don't bump into things and helping them to cross the road. They're also very cute! But the dogs must be specially trained. When Jack gave the dog food in its bowl, for example, he had to blow a whistle before the dog could eat. It was all part of the discipline needed to become a guide dog. Jack loved the responsibility of training dogs. It taught him how important it was to work hard to reach your goal.

Jack played mostly as a scrum-half at first but moved to out-half as he got older. He was a brilliant kicker and spent many long evenings in the field outside his house, trying to send the ball right down the middle of the posts. He practised for hours at the club in Bandon too. Sometimes the coaches had to run him off the pitch when other teams needed to play.

As he neared the age of 18, the hard work started to pay off. Jack and his teammates went on a winning run in the cup. They were a good team, and things were starting to click. They won match after match, upsetting the odds against some bigger sides. Their winning streak saw them go all the way to the All-Ireland Cup Final, where they faced Skerries from Dublin. Nobody gave them a chance. But Jack had other ideas.

Crowley ... A lot of pressure on this young man's shoulders ... He lines up the kick ... And it's straight between the posts. Wow! What a kick. This man has a huge future!

Jack kicked a flawless five from five, playing the game of his life in a 20-7 win.

'Yes, Jacko!' roared his teammate Ciaran.

'We did it!' Jack shouted back as all the players gathered in a circle, jumping up and down and singing.

That performance was one of the reasons he was soon called up for the Ireland under-18s. And from there things started happening quickly. He moved from Bandon to Cork Con to play in the All-Ireland League. Once more he was following in the footsteps of his hero Peter O'Mahony. Then he moved to Munster. And after a couple of short years learning the ropes, he fought his way up to become the starting number 10 for the province.

He soon settled into the role. It seemed the more he played, the better he became. He was improving every week.

Now he faced the biggest test of his career. Munster were playing Leinster in a huge end-of-season game. It was the semi-final of the URC Championship at the Aviva Stadium in Dublin. Leinster had been the best team all year and nobody gave Munster any hope. But just like all those years before when Bandon beat Skerries, Jack believed in his team.

There was a massive crowd in the stadium for this clash between the old rivals. Half in the blue of Leinster and half in the red of Munster. Jack had to pinch himself as he walked onto the pitch behind captain Peter O'Mahony. He still couldn't believe it. He was nervous. But he knew, with Peter on his team, he was in safe hands.

Munster played the better rugby, but a Leinster try from Jason Jenkins left them 10-6 behind at half-time. It was an incredibly tight game. Munster kept going to the end and never gave up. With minutes to go, Leinster were still in the lead by two points. Munster needed to score fast.

Jack and his teammates in red punched the blue defence again and again. But they were gaining only inches. Jack knew it was time to try a drop goal. There was only a second left. They needed 3 points to win it.

Scrum-half Craig Casey was on the ball and Jack let out a roar.

'Yes, Craig!'

He followed the ball as it spun towards him. He caught it perfectly, looked at the posts and in one motion dropped the ball and swung his boot. It was a sweet strike and the ball sailed over the bar.

Ohhhhh, he's got it! Jack Crowley sends the Munster fans to their feet ... that's just like Ronan O'Gara. Munster have a new hero and his name is Jack Crowley!

The Leinster players and fans put their

heads in their hands. Munster had stolen it at the end to win by a single point, 16-15.

'Jack! You pulled it out for us!' said Peter O'Mahony with a smile, as he patted Jack on the head.

'It was a hit and hope!' replied Jack, laughing. But he knew it wasn't. The ball was going over the bar the second he hit it.

Jack and his teammates didn't have much time to celebrate. They were soon on the way to South Africa for the final, where he was about to do it all again. He steered Munster to an epic win over the Stormers, kicking a late conversion from the touchline to seal a 19-14 win. It was Munster's first major title for 12 years.

Crowley with nerves of steel. This boy has the world at his feet!

Munster were back in the big time. And Jack Crowley had shown everyone that he was ready to fill Johnny Sexton's boots.

After his brilliant performances in the red of Munster, Jack was soon wearing the green of Ireland. He got the nod to go to the World Cup in France, where he came off the bench to replace Sexton in three matches. He lapped up every minute he spent in the company of the greatest number 10 ever to play for Ireland. He took note of every detail, from kicking, passing and tackling, to how Johnny urged on his teammates. It was like going to a school for out-halves!

Now, with the new season coming close and Johnny gone, Jack felt he was ready to step up. And so did Andy Farrell. After training one day, he called Jack aside.

'All going well, Jack, you'll be my main man for the Six Nations,' he said.

Jack felt the hairs on the back of his neck stand up.

'Thanks, Andy,' he said.

'Don't thank me,' replied Andy. 'You've earned it with your performances. But remember I've Ross and Harry Byrne and Ciarán Frawley waiting in the wings. Make the most of your opportunity.'

Jack felt such pride in his heart. He was determined not to let anybody down.

Andy had made his big decisions. Ireland were ready to go again. If the team that Andy built was mostly made in Leinster, its beating heart would be from the red blood of Munster. An unlikely blend of rugby royalty made in Cork. Captained by the fiery warrior Peter O'Mahony, with the cool calmness at out-half of young Jack Crowley.

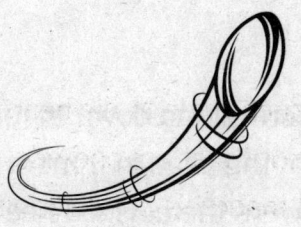

Chapter 5

Young Guns

The television cameras and microphones were switched on. The lights were shining brightly, and all the reporters were ready. They were waiting for Andy Farrell to arrive to break the big news. Today was squad announcement day. The moment when everybody found out who would be selected to play for Ireland in the Six Nations.

The cameras clicked and flashed as Andy entered the room. He waved and smiled to everyone, before sitting down to read the squad list from the page in front of him. All the usual names were there. Hugo Keenan, James Lowe, Bundee Aki, Robbie Henshaw, Garry Ringrose, Jamison Gibson-Park ... Everyone could see now that Andy was sticking with the team that had brought so much success to Ireland. He wasn't about to make a change for the sake of it.

Tadhg Furlong, Dan Sheehan, Andrew Porter ... Andy continued to read from the list. But everyone in the room was getting impatient. They wanted to know the big news. Who was the new captain? Andy had kept it a closely guarded secret.

Tadhg Beirne, James Ryan, Joe McCarthy, Josh van der Flier, Caelan Doris, Jack Conan ... The list went on and on. There were 34 names in total. Each one was honoured to be given the invitation to play for their country. Then finally Andy broke the news.

'Our new captain will be Peter O'Mahony,' he announced. 'He has all the skills and experience we need for the role. And he's the perfect person to lead this group of players on the next stage of their journey.'

Peter walked out to join Andy. He never really enjoyed speaking to the media. But it was easy on a day like this. He smiled for the cameras and answered questions.

'It's an honour and a privilege to be here,' he said in his typical quiet fashion. 'I think there's so much more in this group of players and I'm just dying to get going now.'

'All right, we have to go, Pete!' barked Andy suddenly. Everyone laughed. But Andy was dead serious. 'We've to get training!' said Andy with a smile.

The secret was out. Ireland's new captain had been announced. Now it was time for the work to begin.

The squad assembled at the Irish Rugby Football Union's (IRFU) High Performance Centre in Abbotstown in Dublin. This state-of-the-art facility had everything the players needed to succeed. There was an all-weather indoor pitch, a fully-equipped gym, massage and treatment rooms, video analysis, a canteen where the players could eat together and even a team room to chill out in. It was a home away from home, where they would spend most of their time for the next two months.

***

Ireland's first Six Nations game against France was just weeks away. It was going to be a tough one. Only a few months had passed since Ireland lost their World Cup quarter-final to the All Blacks in Paris. Now they were heading back to France once more.

France had also lost their quarter-final at the World Cup to the eventual winners, South Africa. So they too were out for revenge. To make it even more interesting, the game had been moved to Marseille in the south of France, where a noisy crowd was waiting for them. It wasn't going to be easy for Ireland. Especially after they got bad news on the injury front.

Young Guns

Winger Mack Hansen had been one of the stars of the World Cup. He was as quick as lightning and a tricky, skilful runner. When he got going, he was almost impossible to catch. He was fun away from the pitch too, always laughing, joking and playing tricks on his teammates. He had scored nine tries in 21 appearances for Ireland since he first came into the side and was one of the first names on the team sheet when Andy Farrell picked his starting 15.

Not long before the beginning of the Six Nations, Mack was playing for Connacht in a big clash against Munster. With the game in the balance, he caught a high ball and began one of his trademark runs. He jinked left and right before looking for a bit of space. Suddenly, a Munster defender came out of nowhere with a heavy hit.

Owwwww!

Mack went down, clutching his shoulder. The physio and doctor ran straight onto the pitch to check him out. It didn't look good. The physio broke the news.

'It looks like it's dislocated,' he said, as he strapped up Mack's arm in a sling.

'How long will I be out for?' asked Mack as he scrunched up his face in pain.

'Four months at least,' said the physio. 'I'm sorry, Mack.'

Mack dropped his head in his hands. He knew he was going to miss the Six Nations. He wanted to cry.

Andy felt the same when he heard the news. Mack was one of the most important players on the team. But now he had to plan without him. And, just a short time later, the injury curse struck again.

Centre Garry Ringrose was playing an important Champions Cup match for Leinster against the English team Leicester. Garry was another one of Andy's key players. He was a certain starter and his experience was crucial to the team. But, just like Mack, Garry took a heavy blow to the shoulder.

Owwwwww!

The news wasn't quite as bad as Mack's. His

shoulder wasn't dislocated. He wasn't ruled out of the whole Six Nations. But he was going to miss the first match against France. The problems were piling up for Andy and his coaches.

Luckily for Andy, he had plenty of other strong players to choose from. On the wing, he had Jacob Stockdale, Jordan Larmour and Calvin Nash. Nash was a hard-working winger from Limerick who had waited a long time for his big break. He had been in and out of the Munster team over the years and had never really made a place in the team his own. But over the last season he had really started to click. He was one of the standout players, alongside Jack Crowley, as Munster won the United Rugby Championship title in South Africa. Now, at the age of 27, he was on the verge of his first Six Nations start for Ireland.

The centre was well stocked too, with Bundee Aki, Robbie Henshaw and Stuart McCloskey. Competition for places in the team was fierce and the players worked hard to make sure they were picked.

Another player putting his hand up for selection was Joe McCarthy. 'Big Joe' as Andy called him. Just two years earlier he hadn't even played for Leinster. Now he was close to starting for Ireland in the Six Nations.

Joe was born in New York, USA. His dad was from Castletownbere in West Cork and his mam was from Cashel in Tipperary. But he had lived most of his life in Dublin. So, despite his Munster blood, he was a true-blue Leinsterman. He played rugby for Willow Park, Blackrock and Trinity. But back when he was a teenager, nobody ever thought he would one day play for Ireland. Not even Joe himself.

He was considered small for a player in his position in the second row and he was often only picked for the fourth team in school. But he loved the game, and he kept showing up every week, even if he wasn't in the starting team. He trained hard and took all the advice he could get. As he got older, he started to grow too, eventually reaching six feet six inches. When he finished school, he went to

Trinity College to study business. He joined the rugby team while he was there and, suddenly, things started to happen for him.

His confidence grew with every match he played. He got a run for the team in the All-Ireland League, where his performances caught the eye of Leinster. Within a few months, he was training for Leinster and eventually made it to the starting team. It was a remarkable rise to the top. Even Joe was taken by surprise. He had only played 28 times for Leinster and was still studying for his college exams when he was picked for the Ireland World Cup squad. That was a shock. But now, he was possibly about to start his first Six Nations game for Ireland. His head was spinning.

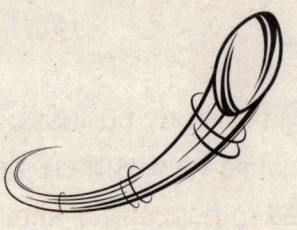

Chapter 6

Portugal Preparations

Big Joe, Jack, Calvin and the other young guns joined the squad as they flew out to Portugal for a warm-weather training camp. It was just a week before the tournament started. A chance to do some last-minute work on their skills and tactics as the first game against France drew near.

It was nice for the players to get away from the winter weather in Ireland. On Wednesday, it was time for Andy to pick his team. He called them into the dressing room.

'Make no mistake, boys,' he said in his clear, calm voice. 'This is a huge game. Going down to the south of France to take on this team is not going to be easy.'

The players listened intently to every word he said. Captain Peter O'Mahony sat at the front of the room, rubbing his hands together. He could already feel the tension building. It was just the way he liked it before a big match.

'We've picked the team we think can beat this French side. We have trust in all of you. It's not just the starting 15, or the match day 22. It's about the whole squad. Keeping each other honest. Pushing each other every day. We have something special going on here and I'm so proud of every one of you, whether you make the team or not,' said Andy.

Jack Crowley took a deep breath. He had been given the nod by Andy. But you're never sure until your name is on the team sheet. It was a huge moment for him. Big Joe McCarthy tapped his foot nervously on the ground.

He hoped he had done enough in training
to convince Andy and forwards coach Paul
O'Connell that he was good enough to start.
And Calvin Nash could feel sweat building on
the palms of his hands. He was so close to
that starting jersey he could almost feel it. He
prayed this would be his day.

Andy read out the team. 'Number 15 Hugo
Keenan ... Number 13 Robbie Henshaw ...
Number 12 Bundee Aki ... Number 11 James
Lowe ... Number 9 Jamison Gibson-Park ...
Number 1 Andrew Porter ... Number 2 Dan
Sheehan ... Number 3 Tadhg Furlong ...
Number 5 Tadhg Beirne ... Number 7 Josh van
der Flier ... Number 8 Caelan Doris.'

Andy took a moment and smiled. 'And a
special mention for the following players,'
he said as he looked up and scanned the
room. 'Number 6 ... Our new captain, Peter
O'Mahony ... And, making their first Six
Nations starts ... Number 4 Big Joe McCarthy
... Number 10 Jack Crowley ... And Number 14
Calvin Nash.'

Portugal Preparations

Peter was thrilled. It was now official. He was about to lead his national team out as captain in a huge Six Nations clash against France.

Jack could feel butterflies in his stomach. All his life had been leading to this moment. Now it was real. He was about to take the reins from Johnny Sexton as Ireland's new out-half. Joe still couldn't believe it. In just two years he had come from college rugby at Trinity to a Six Nations start. And Calvin was grinning from ear to ear. He had done it. He had got the nod to start on the wing.

'It's a huge opportunity for you all,' said Andy. 'Now go and make the most of it!'

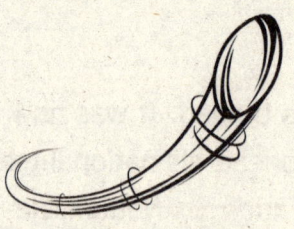

Chapter 7

Marseille

The noise was deafening inside the Stade Velodrome in Marseille. It was a Friday night under lights, a very special occasion, and the fans were doing everything they could to play their part. France usually played all their home games in Paris. But because the Olympic Games were on in the French capital later that year, the game was moved to Marseille.

It was a real treat for the locals to see the French team play in their city. They were determined to make the most of it. They arrived early with their faces painted in blue, white and red, like the French flag. They sang and cheered, and some even brought trumpets. As they waited in the tunnel, the Irish players were surrounded by a wall of noise. It was like nothing they had ever heard before.

'OK, let's go!' said the referee from the back of the tunnel. The players moved forward as one. This was it.

Peter O'Mahony led the team out onto the pitch. The stadium was spectacular. A futuristic bowl that looked like a spaceship. The floodlights dazzled his eyes and all he could see was a sea of blue. He could hardly pick out any Irish fans and he certainly couldn't hear them.

The crowd quietened briefly as they got ready for the national anthems. Then the noise rose again as they sang 'La Marseillaise', the French national anthem, with all their might. There were 76,000 voices passionately singing one of the great anthems in the world. Then it was time for 'Ireland's Call'. The Irish players lined up and put their arms around each other's shoulders.

Peter closed his eyes as he passionately sang. 'Come the day and come the hour ...' This was the moment he had dreamed of since he was a child. Leading his country on to the biggest stage of all.

Big Joe sang proudly too, his arms tightly wound around Caelan Doris. Jack Crowley felt shivers down his spine. But strangely he wasn't nervous. He felt ready. Calvin Nash jumped up and down as the anthem ended. He just wanted the game to start!

Once the anthems were over, the referee blew his whistle.

'Let's go, Jack!' roared Peter O'Mahony as he clapped his hands, waiting for Jack Crowley to kick off.

It took a while for the players to settle. It was so noisy, neither side could hear the calls. They were roaring instructions, but nobody could hear inside this cauldron of a stadium.

Ireland seemed to settle first. Soon Jack Crowley had his first shot on goal. The pressure was on. But he kept calm, taking deep breaths and going through his familiar routine. When he was ready, he lined up the ball. Stepped back and then went for it. He knew as soon as it left his boot that it was a clean strike.

Crowley. With his first Six Nations points on offer. He gets them!

3-0 Ireland. Just the start they wanted.

Then it got even better. France made a strangely slow start to the game. And Ireland took full advantage. They were flying at France from all over the pitch. Soon, they scored again.

Bundee Aki ... to Gibson-Park ... Can they make it?! Yes they can! Tryyyyy! Ireland in for the first try of the 2024 Six Nations. Created by Aki. Finished by Gibson-Park!

Jack Crowley calmly kicked the conversion. He felt on top of the world. From the re-start, he got his hands on the ball once more. He loved getting some space to show his skills.

Even in the heat of a Six Nations battle, it felt just like he was playing for his local club Bandon as a boy.

Crowley. Passes it to Tadhg Beirne, who finds a huge hole.

Tryyyyy!

Where oh where did the French defence go?!

Ireland were 17-3 up after half an hour.

Then luck went their way again. French forward Paul Willemse made a clumsy tackle on Caelan Doris. It was high and dangerous. His second bad tackle of the match. The referee had no choice but to send him off.

A red card! France are down to 14 men!

Peter gathered the players into a huddle.

'Keep calm, boys!' he roared. 'These French lads are always dangerous!'

And he was right. Just before half-time they struck back.

France are coming ... France are coming ... Penaud ... Damian Penaud!

Tryyyyy!

The French were back in the game, right before half-time. The score was 17-10 now. Game on.

'Brilliant start, boys!' said Andy, as he patted his players on the back on their way into the dressing room. 'Remember your detail. Keep going. We've made a super start. But that's all. These guys only need a second to score a try,' he said, as the players drank energy drinks and iced their tired muscles.

The second half was even more exciting. France threw everything at Ireland. Their captain Grégory Alldritt made a powerful run. He was normally unstoppable. But Big Joe had other ideas.

Smassshhhhhh!

Joe nailed him with a perfect tackle. The green wall held firm again.

Now it was Ireland's turn to attack. Once more they made the most of it. They fired the ball quickly out to the backs and across the pitch, fizzing quick passes to each other to move the French around. In a flash the ball came to Calvin Nash on the wing.

Doris ... Out wide ... Nash!

Tryyyyy!

Calvin Nash crosses over for his first Six Nations try. He's in dreamland!

'Yes, Nashy!' screamed Peter with delight. He was starting to believe Ireland might hold out to win. But France responded again with a try of their own.

Every time Ireland throw a punch, France throw another one!

It was 24-17 now. Ireland remained in front but only by one score.

They were getting tired. But Jack Crowley continued to drive the team on. It was up to him whether to run with the ball, pass or kick. The pressure was huge, but he was loving every minute. He fired another perfect penalty straight down the line. Ireland had a lineout in a great position.

Hooker Dan Sheehan wiped the ball with a towel to dry it. Tadhg Beirne made the lineout call. This was what all the practice was for. Sheehan threw the ball high into the air. Big Joe jumped like a spring, as Tadhg Furlong lifted him as high as he could. Joe snatched the ball cleanly and fired it down to Josh van der Flier. Without anyone noticing, Josh flicked the ball back to Sheehan, who had tucked in behind. Suddenly the Irish team powered over the line.

Tryyyyy!

It's the bonus point try from Dan Sheehan. Surely now a rare victory on French soil is within their grasp!

France knew the game was up. And right before the end, Rónan Kelleher crossed the try line once more.

Tryyyyy! A statement win for Ireland in France!

The referee blew the full-time whistle. Ireland had done it. A huge 38-17 win. The most points ever scored by an Irish team in France. Nobody had seen that coming.

'Yeahhhhhhh!' roared Peter O'Mahony with the last bit of energy he had in his body.

It was an incredible performance from the three players making their first Six Nations starts. Jack Crowley kicked a superb six from seven. Calvin Nash scored a try. And Big Joe McCarthy was named man of the match.

Peter gathered the three of them together on the pitch.

'Remember this moment,' he said. 'Take it all in. These days don't come around too often in this game. You deserve it after all the hard work. Enjoy it!'

The players high-fived each other. It was a moment none of them would ever forget.

Inside the dressing room, Andy was as proud as punch. But he quickly brought the players back down to earth.

'I'm so proud you kept going for the full 80 minutes,' he said. 'We got what we deserved today. But remember we've won nothing yet. There are four more games to come. We need to back up that performance next week.'

Peter joined in. 'A special word for the young fellas,' he said, trying to get some silence as the players danced and sang in the dressing room. 'Nashy, Jack and Big Joe. Some big, big performances from guys getting an opportunity.'

He led the players in three cheers.

'Hip Hip ... Hooray!

Hip Hip ... Hooray!

Hip Hip ... Hooray!'

Ireland had survived their toughest task in that year's Six Nations. They had come up with one of the all-time great performances in Irish rugby history. They'd shown everyone that they had overcome their World Cup heartbreak. That there was life after Johnny Sexton. And that their young stars were ready for the big time.

It was the perfect start to the Six Nations. A night of Marseille magic.

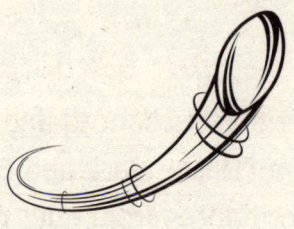

Chapter 8

Lowe Lie the Fields

If the beating heart of the Ireland team came from the red of Munster, then its power and pace was forged on the rugby fields of New Zealand. James Lowe had long been a skilful and speedy winger, scoring tries for fun for Leinster and Ireland. Now he had reached another level, adding great defence to his game to become an all-round superstar winger. One of the best in the game. But as a young boy in New Zealand, he had thought his rugby dreams might never come true.

James Francis Rawiri Lowe was born on 8 July 1992 in Nelson, New Zealand. He was the youngest of three kids in a sporty family. His mam Yvonne was an excellent netball player. His dad loved rugby, where he played on the wing. His sister Charlene played netball for New Zealand while she was in school. So it was no surprise that James loved all sports as a kid. He played cricket, volleyball and football. He won athletics competitions, especially in shot put, and even played basketball for the national team. He was a real all-rounder. But, like his dad, rugby was his favourite.

But when he was 14, everything changed for James. One day, he noticed a rash on his body. He didn't think too much about it. But then he started to get sicker and sicker very quickly. Within a few months, he couldn't get out of bed. His parents were very worried. Some days he found it hard to even walk to the toilet or eat his dinner without help. James seemed to have lost all his strength. He went to see different doctors but none of them could figure out what was wrong with him. James thought his dreams of playing professional rugby were over for good. All he wanted was to walk normally again and play with his friends.

After many tests and visits to the doctor, James was diagnosed with arthritis, an illness that makes your joints stiff and sore. He spent time in hospital and the doctors tried lots of different treatments to help him. None of them seemed to work. James was so upset. He just wanted to be a normal teenager again. He wanted to go to school, play sports and hang out with his friends. It seemed that the life he knew and loved was slipping away. Then, one day, out of the blue, he had a breakthrough.

'We might have some good news,' said the doctor, as James sat on the hospital bed with his mam and dad by his side. 'There's a new medicine available and we think it might just work for you.'

James was thrilled. 'Here's hoping, Doc!' he said with a smile.

Lowe Lie the Fields

Within weeks James started taking the medicine. And in no time at all he began to get better. He was over the moon. It took him a long time to get back his strength. He had lost a lot of weight and missed a lot of training. But slowly and surely, he fought his way back to health. Walking at first, then running, then playing with a ball. Taking it step by step. Finally, he was ready to get back on the pitch. From then on, there was no stopping him.

James was determined to make up for lost time. He trained harder than all the other boys. He wasn't going to waste his second chance. He was picked for New Zealand's national schools' team, and eventually his province, Tasman Mako. It wasn't long before his performances there saw him picked up by Super Rugby side the Chiefs, one of the biggest clubs in New Zealand. It was an amazing journey from his sickbed to Super Rugby. But his adventure was only just beginning.

James was picked four times for the Maori All Blacks. It was a huge honour for him and his family. But he was unable to find his way into the New Zealand team. Then one day he got a phone call from the other side of the world that changed his life. It was Leinster coach Leo Cullen.

'James, Leo Cullen here,' he said on the phone.

'Leo who?' thought James to himself.

'We've been impressed by your performances, and we've put together a great offer for you. How do you fancy moving to Dublin? You're exactly what we need,' said Leo, trying to convince James to take the leap.

James didn't have to think long about it. Within days, he signed for Leinster, ready to start a new life in the northern hemisphere.

***

James settled in Leinster almost straight away. Dublin already felt like home. And right from the start it showed on the pitch. In his first

game, Leinster were playing Italian team
Benetton, and it took just 16 minutes for
James to make an impact.

**Leinster driving forward ... McGrath ...
Pops it to Lowe ...**

Tryyyyy!

**James Lowe touches down on his
debut!**

He high-fived his teammates as he pulled
back his long, wavy black hair. He hadn't yet
started to wear his famous ponytail. That
would come later. And, before the end of the
match, he scored another try. It was a sight
Leinster fans would get used to over the next
few years, as James touched down try after
try. He won four United Rugby Championship
(URC) titles in his first four years at Leinster
and the European Rugby Champions Cup. It
was the stuff of dreams!

After three years in his adopted country,
James was now allowed to play for Ireland. His
first match was against Wales in the 2020 Six
Nations. He quickly became a regular starter in

the team and the following year came his most special moment in the green jersey.

Ireland played the All Blacks in a November test match at the Aviva Stadium. It was a huge honour for James to play for Ireland against his homeland. His family were unable to travel over for the special day but James gave them plenty to cheer, as they watched at home on television. It was a sparkling night in Dublin, with an electric atmosphere inside the Aviva Stadium. James was quick into the action.

Fast ball from right to left ... Hugo Keenan ... to Looooowe ...

Tryyyyy!

James Lowe, against his home country, puts Ireland in front!

'Yes, Lowey!' roared Josh van der Flier as he crashed over.

The game was an absolute classic. Both sides threw everything at it. James put in a huge defensive effort, alongside every one of his teammates. In the end, Ireland held on for a 29-10 win. It was one of the all-time great Irish performances.

It took Ireland 111 years to beat the All Blacks. Now they've done it three times in five years!

The crowd burst into song, with a stirring rendition of the 'Fields of Athenry'. 'Low lie the Fields of Athenry ...'

'They're singing my song, bro!' said James as he high-fived Hugo Keenan.

'Eh, I don't think so,' replied Hugo, laughing at James.

'For sure, man. "Lowe lie the fields!" That's my name!' said James with a smile, as he waved to the crowd.

It was a hugely proud moment for James and his family. He called them after the game.

'You did it, son!' said his dad. He was so proud he wore an Ireland jersey around their hometown in New Zealand for weeks after the win.

'I'm so proud of you,' said his mam, with tears in her eyes. 'I wish I could give you a hug!'

Ireland's Call

It was hard for them all to imagine that just over ten years before, James was in hospital thinking he would never play rugby again. Now he was a star in the making for his adopted country of Ireland.

'Never in a million years did I think this would happen. Life can be strange!' he said to his mam and dad.

He had travelled a long way. But he knew there was still much more to come on his journey in the green jersey of Ireland.

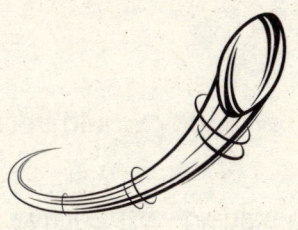

Chapter 9

Dan the Man

While James Lowe was scoring tries for fun as a schoolboy in New Zealand, Dan Sheehan was making his own way in the rugby world back in Dublin. Like many of his teammates with Ireland and Leinster, Dan came from a strong rugby background. His grandad played for Clontarf and Leinster way back in the 1950s, while his dad, Barry, played for University College Dublin and Old Belvedere. So it was only natural that Dan and his younger brother Bobby would become rugby players too.

Dan began playing with Bective minis at the age of five. He was big for his age even then. And he took rugby very seriously too. He was never one for laughing and joking when he was on the pitch. He loved playing rugby, but that all changed one day when he was 11, when his dad came home from work to break some news.

'I've been offered the chance to move for my job,' he told Dan, Bobby and their younger sisters Emma and Susie. 'We're heading for a new adventure in Romania!'

It was a shock to Dan at first, but he and his family were excited about the move. It was something totally new and it was only for a few years. But it meant no more rugby for Dan for a while.

He settled well into his new life at school in Romania. It was very different, but he loved it. He tried all kinds of sports, including football, badminton, athletics and swimming. He enjoyed it so much he was named athlete of the year in his first year at the school. And he kept up his rugby skills playing in the garden with his brother. He practised his lineout throwing until his arms got tired. Or until their mam called them in for dinner.

A few years later Dan moved back to Ireland, where he started at Clongowes Wood Secondary School. He was a big strong hooker, with a great lineout throw. All those years of practice had paid off! And he was fast too. Unusually fast for a hooker. But sometimes he lacked confidence. He didn't always believe in himself.

At the beginning, he was selected for the second team. He worked hard and listened to his coaches and continued to improve. Eventually, he made it onto the school Senior Cup team and played in two Senior Cup semi-finals. It was at Clongowes that he first showed off his trademark move, peeling off the back of a lineout to sprint over the try line. He was a very good player but, at the time, nobody ever thought he would become a future star.

After school, he moved on to play for

Lansdowne in the All Ireland League and
at college with Trinity. At first, he struggled
with the step up to senior level. He found the
scrums really tough, coming up against bigger,
stronger men. But he was a fast learner and
soon got up to speed. And it wasn't long before
he was called up to play for Leinster. He had
improved a lot in a short space of time. But
there was much more to come.

Most players just want to survive their first
match in the blue of Leinster. To show they can
compete at the top level. But not Dan Sheehan.
He burst onto the scene in a thumping 63-8
win over Zebre, scoring two tries in his first
ever match. Leinster knew they had something
special on their hands. He had grown into a
man now. Standing six feet three inches tall and
weighing a whopping 17 stone. He kept all his
trademark speed too. That mixture of power
and pace made him a nightmare for defences
to stop. After the match, Leinster coach Stuart
Lancaster called Dan aside.

'Some game, Dan!' he said, as he patted

him on the back. 'You can go all the way. Just keep believing in yourself!'

It was a huge boost for Dan, who hadn't always believed he was good enough to reach the top. Now, he felt there was nothing stopping him.

He lit up the URC season for Leinster, becoming a try machine. He even scored four tries in one match. Unheard of for a hooker! He was re-inventing the role. His flying form quickly caught the eye of Andy Farrell and he was soon wearing the green shirt.

Dan made his first appearance for Ireland in a November international win against Japan at the Aviva Stadium. By the time the Six Nations rolled around, he had become a regular in the matchday squad. Then an injury to first-choice hooker Rónan Kelleher opened the door for his first time in the starting lineup. Dan, as ever, took his chance with both hands, playing his part in a win over Italy. In the next match against Scotland, he showed everyone what he could do, scoring a terrific try.

Ireland's Call

Ireland won 26-5 to collect the Triple Crown and Dan was named player of the match. He seemed to improve every time he played.

The following year, things got even better. Ireland were hunting down Grand Slam success in the Six Nations and took on England in their final game at the Aviva Stadium. It was a huge match. The biggest Dan had ever played. The stadium was packed with 50,000 fans hoping to see history.

Dan stood with his teammates for the anthems, his legs shaking with emotion. The whistle blew and the game was on. Dan looked around and took a deep breath. He was about to play a starring role in one of the most memorable days in Irish rugby history.

Ireland made a nervous start and England went in front. But they worked their way back into the game and soon had an attacking lineout. Dan knew exactly what to do. It was the same move he had perfected back at school in Clongowes. He threw the ball in, just as he had practised as a kid in his garden back in

Romania. It was a perfect spiral high into the air and came back out to flanker Josh van der Flier. Dan put his head down and stepped on the gas.

Van der Flier ... Back inside ... Gap opens up ... Sheehannnnnnnn! Ireland have the opening try and the place has gone wild!

Robbie Henshaw added another try in the second half, but with just over ten minutes to play the game remained in the balance. Ireland were running out of energy. But they were in front and were pushing for a try to kill the game.

Conan ... To Sheehan in the corner ... Dan Sheehannnnnnn! That. Is. Wonderful. Jack Conan the creator ... Sheehan finished like a winger. Ireland have their third try and surely the Grand Slam is in the bag!

Dan let out a huge roar. 'Yesssssss!' he screamed, as his teammates piled on top of him.

'Dano the Mano!' roared Mack Hansen into Dan's ear as the fans erupted in celebration.

They had done it. Ireland had won the Grand Slam and Dan Sheehan was the hero. His two tries helped them to a famous win and he was named man of the match. It didn't get much better than this.

All his family were there to watch and they celebrated with him afterwards. His dad Barry gave him a huge hug as the floodlights twinkled above the Aviva Stadium.

'I always knew you could do it, son,' he said, with a tear in his eye.

'You were with me all the way, Dad. I couldn't have done it without you,' said Dan, a smile on his face. He thought of his long journey from Bective minis, to Romania, to Clongowes, Trinity and Lansdowne. To Leinster and then Ireland. He never really believed he was good enough to make it all the way. But now here he was. A Grand Slam champion. Scorer of two tries. Man of the match. It was everything he had ever dreamed of.

But he was still young and he was hungry for much more success.

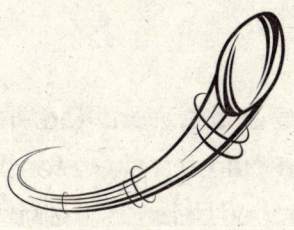

Chapter 10

The Italian Job

After the famous night in Marseille, Andy
Farrell had a job to do keeping the players' feet
on the ground. Yes, it was a huge win. But it
was only their first game of the championship.
There was still a long way to go. Dan Sheehan
and James Lowe played their part in an
extraordinary night for Irish rugby and they
were raring to go for the next match against
Italy at the Aviva Stadium. All the players
were. It was their first home game since the

disappointment at the World Cup in France and they wanted to put on a show for the fans.

But the story of Ireland's match against Italy didn't begin on a Sunday in February at the Aviva Stadium. It began a few months before in the unusual place of a television studio at RTÉ and the annual Christmas *Late Late Toy Show*.

The Toy Show is one of the biggest nights of the year in Ireland, when all the children sit down for a special night of entertainment. It's a chance to see all the latest toys before they write their list for Santa. This year, it was an extra special night for one lucky boy, seven-year-old Stevie Mulrooney from Kilkenny. He was invited onto the show to sing his favourite song, 'Ireland's Call', the anthem of the Irish rugby team.

He joined presenter Patrick Kielty on the show, dressed from head to toe in his full Ireland kit. As he began the song, little did he know he was in for a special surprise. He put his hand on his heart and sang with all his might.

Come the day and come the hour …
Come the power and the glory …

The audience clapped along and joined in.

Ireland … Ireland … Together
standing tall.

Just then, behind his back, out walked Peter O'Mahony and Bundee Aki. Stevie looked around with shock on his face. His two heroes were standing right beside him as he sang.

Shoulder to shoulder … We'll answer
Ireland's Call!

Stevie's eyes opened wide with delight as he finished his performance. Bundee patted him on the back and Peter shook his hand.

'This is the best day of my life,' said Stevie with a smile. But his adventure didn't end there. A short time later, Stevie got a video call from Josh van der Flier.

'I hear you're coming along to the Italy game,' said Josh as he sat in the Ireland changing room.

'Yeah,' replied Stevie, almost unable to speak with excitement.

'Well, we've heard your singing voice,' continued Josh. 'And we'd love for you to lead "Ireland's Call" for us at the game.'

'Oh wow!' said Stevie with a smile. 'I'd love to do that for my nation!'

So, a few months later, when the Ireland players took to the field against Italy for their second match of the Six Nations, they were led out by the luckiest seven-year-old boy in the country.

Stevie stood proud in front of 50,000 fans, with another million or so watching on television back home. If he was nervous, he didn't show it. He belted out the song with all the passion he had shown on the *Late Late Toy Show*.

Ireland ... Ireland ... Together standing tall ...

The Ireland players stood shoulder-to-shoulder as Stevie sang. Josh van der Flier, Bundee Aki and Peter O'Mahony. James Lowe and Dan Sheehan. They stood in line singing their anthem, backed by the fans in the stadium and watching at home. It was a show of unity and strength. A special moment. Stevie finished the song to a huge cheer. He smiled and waved. Instantly, everyone in the stadium knew that Ireland just weren't going to lose today.

Andy Farrell watched from the coaches' box.

'He's special, that kid,' he said to Paul O'Connell. 'I hope our players show as much bottle as he just did!'

But there was no need for Andy to worry. Ireland were simply sensational from start to finish. Italy didn't stand a chance.

Ireland began the scoring after just five minutes. Hugo Keenan made a darting run from his own 22-metre line to get Ireland on the front foot. The players knew immediately that they were on the attack and passed the ball out wide with pace. Within seconds, out-half Jack Crowley had his hands on the ball.

Crowley the creator shows his dancing feet ... Pops it to Nash ... To Casey ... Back to Crowley who's through the gap ... Tryyyyy! Jack Crowley with his first international try!

'Some skills, Jacko!' said Calvin Nash, as Jack smiled from ear to ear.

Before long, Ireland were in again. Their attack was on fire, with Jack Crowley fanning the flames.

Crowley ... great hands ... Oh, wonderful ... McCloskey ... Sheehan ... Tryyyyy! That was a thing of beauty ... The finish from Sheehan, but what about that from Crowley? Masterful from the young man.

'Great stuff, Dano!' roared Jack Crowley, as Dan Sheehan rose to his feet.

'Not so bad yourself, Jack!' replied Dan with a grin. 'You're doing a fine job filling Johnny Sexton's boots!'

Just before half-time, Ireland added another try. It was one-way traffic. This time Jack Conan crashed over from a lineout. They led 19-0 at the break. Things were looking good.

'Great stuff, boys!' roared Andy Farrell in the dressing room at half-time. 'Lovely attack! But I'm more proud of the defence. It's not often you keep a team to nil. Be proud of that and keep going!'

Soon after the restart, Dan Sheehan was back in the thick of the action. It was a typical lineout move, but the Italian defence just switched off and Dan waltzed in to score.

The maul begins to rumble ... Sheehan should be there ... and is there ... Tryyyyy! Ireland have the bonus point!

'That's the easiest try you'll ever get!' joked James Ryan.

'If it's so easy, why don't you do it?' said Dan with a laugh.

The players were enjoying it, and so were the fans. There was a party atmosphere in the stadium. Soon, they witnessed something extra special. A James Lowe wonder try.

James Lowe gets the ball ... Turns on the gas ... Swats away three Italian defenders ... Five metres ... Three metres ... One metre ... Tryyyyy! James Lowe stretches out a long arm to touch the ball down for try number five for Ireland!

There was still time for one more try. Calvin Nash touched down in the closing seconds to put the icing on the cake of a 36-0 win. Ireland had made it two wins in a row.

James Lowe was named man of the match after a sensational display. He looked around the stadium as the fans sang his name, tying his hair back in his trademark ponytail. It was a moment he could never have dreamed of when he was in his sick bed as a teenager back home in New Zealand, struggling with arthritis. He was so grateful for the life Ireland had given him, and the love and support of the fans in his adopted country.

Andrew Porter joined him and squeezed him in a bear hug, lifting him into the air.

'Let's go!' he roared. He was on top of the world. And Ireland were top of the Six Nations table.

'Right, boys, let's not get too carried away!' said Andy Farrell, bringing them back down to earth with a bang in the changing room afterwards.

'Nice tries. Good performance, but plenty of stuff to work on. Lowey, you played well. But our scrum was man of the match. And you should be very proud of keeping Italy to nil. That doesn't happen often in international rugby. Let's stay focused. The competition only gets going now.'

It was a great speech. The players really believed they were on to something special as a group. They felt nothing would stop them now.

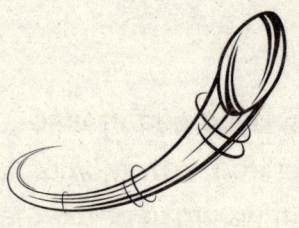

Chapter 11

Bundee

Just like James Lowe, Bundee Aki's journey to play for Ireland began on the other side of the world. He arrived at the Ireland training camp on the Monday before their next game against Wales and went to the team room for breakfast. He prepared his usual meal before training. Six Weetabix, a bagel and a banana. The breakfast of champions, he liked to call it. As he waited for his coffee to brew, his mind wandered back over the long journey he had made, from a schoolboy in New Zealand, to becoming a star of Irish rugby.

Fua Leiofi Bundellu Aki, or Bundee for short, was born on 7 April 1990, in Auckland, New Zealand. His parents, Hercules and Sautia, were from Samoa, a small island nation in the middle of the South Pacific Ocean. His parents made their life in New Zealand, where they had six children. Bundee was the second oldest of two boys and four girls. At an early age, he learned that family was the most important thing in the world.

His hometown in South Auckland was a tough place to grow up. It was a poor place and there wasn't much for young people to do. Luckily for Bundee, he fell in love with a game that would change the course of his life. From the first time he picked up a rugby ball, he knew it was for him. And it helped that he was quite good at it, too.

Bundee wasn't very big as a young boy. But he was tough. He had heaps of energy and was always looking for a bit of mischief. He found it hard to concentrate in school and was a real messer. He was always getting in trouble with his teachers at Manurewa High School. But when he stepped onto the rugby pitch, it was a different story. He felt at home. He threw himself into tackles and loved taking on the bigger boys. They usually came off worse.

His coaches knew he was talented, but he needed a bit of work. He wasn't the best at taking instructions and he didn't always live life away from the pitch as he should. He was often caught eating treats that were bad for him and he sometimes missed training too. But when he was switched on, he was as good as anyone.

At the age of 16, he was offered a chance to move to a school in England to study and play rugby. It was a life-changing experience and he jumped at the chance. He was still a handful for the teachers at school, but he worked hard in England and learned as much as he could on the rugby pitch. Away from the game though, he found it hard to be so far from his family, especially at Christmas, so he went back as often as he could.

Then, one day, he got some surprising news. He was going to become a father. So he packed his bags in England and moved back home to Auckland for the birth of his first daughter. It changed everything for Bundee. He had to grow up fast. He was a man now and had a family to support. No more messing around with rugby, he thought. He needed to get a proper job.

He worked as a builder for a while and then got a job in a bank. It was a tough time in his life. He woke up at 6 a.m. to train before work. Then he worked all day in the bank before trying to fit in more rugby in the evening. He was watching his friends having fun and moving up in the rugby world, while he was working full-time and looking after his family. He thought his rugby dreams had gone forever. But then he got the break he'd been dreaming of.

He was offered a contract with Super Rugby club, the Chiefs. They were one of the best clubs in New Zealand, with players like Sonny Bill Williams in their team. Bundee realised this was the chance he had always wanted, and he wasn't going to waste it. He worked as hard as he could. He trained like his life depended on it. He ate all the right food. And he made sure he slept properly every night. He gave 100 per cent in every match and listened to every word of advice from coaches and senior players. There was no more messing. Things were serious now.

And soon the rewards came. He fought his way into the first team, where he won back-to-back Super Rugby titles. He was making waves and many people said he would play for the All Blacks one day. But then he received a call that would change his life.

Pat Lam was another well-known New Zealander who had a Samoan background. He was the coach of Connacht and had heard all about the young Bundee Aki, tearing it up in Super Rugby back in New Zealand. He decided to give him a ring.

Bundee

'How do you fancy a trip to the other side of the world?' he said to Bundee on the phone. 'I want you to come to Galway and play for me in Connacht. I want to build a new team around you. It'll be an adventure!'

Bundee wasn't sure at first. 'I don't even know where Galway is,' he said to Pat.

But he soon made the decision to take a leap and move to Ireland. His family was growing, he had two children now, and the money on offer was good. He could raise his family in Ireland and have a better life than the one he had in New Zealand. It was too good to turn down, he thought. It turned out to be the best decision of his life.

***

Bundee settled much better on the other side of the world the second time around. He instantly clicked with Pat Lam and his new teammates. And he soon fell in love with Galway, even if it rained too much. That meant he quickly found his feet on the rugby pitch and soon the

Connacht fans were mad about their new star. He had skills, power and pace. But what they admired more than anything was his bravery. He never took a backwards step.

Bundee didn't change who he was away from the pitch. He still loved having fun in the dressing room. He was always the first to play tricks on his teammates and be in on the jokes. But when it came to training and matches, he became deadly serious. His hard work soon rubbed off on his teammates, who followed his lead to improve their performances.

Before long, Connacht were transformed as a team. With Pat Lam in charge, Bundee in midfield, rising stars Robbie Henshaw and Finlay Bealham in their ranks, and club legends Tiernan O'Halloran and John Muldoon leading the way, they became a match for anyone. And, to the surprise of everyone in the rugby world, they won the league title in Bundee's second year, beating their bigger rivals Leinster, Munster and Ulster along the way.

Bundee

Bundee's family joined him in Ireland and they made their home in Oranmore, just outside Galway. After three years, he was allowed to play for Ireland. Joe Schmidt was the coach at the time and he jumped at the chance to pick Bundee.

He came straight into the team on his first start against South Africa in a November international. Right away, the Irish fans could see what everyone in Connacht already knew. Bundee was something special. His bulk and bravery added something extra that Ireland had been missing. In a few short months in the green jersey, he played a crucial role in Ireland winning the Grand Slam. He played in every match and scored tries against Italy and Wales. They were the first of many in a green shirt.

***

Over the next few years, Bundee became one of the most important players in the Ireland team. One of the highlights was playing his part as Ireland beat his home country, New Zealand, for the first time on home soil. A couple of years later it was time for the re-match, this time in New Zealand. Ireland had never won a test series there. It was the hardest place in world rugby to go and win. Andy Farrell and his players targeted this tour to lay down a marker ahead of the World Cup. For Bundee, it was extra special. For many of his family and friends, it would be their first chance to see him play live in the green shirt of Ireland. It made him so proud.

The first test match in his hometown of Auckland didn't go too well. Ireland put up a good fight but lost 42-19. They learned some valuable lessons, though, and in the following week, they got their revenge. Andrew Porter scored two tries, as Ireland beat the All Blacks in New Zealand for the first time ever. Now it all came down to the final match in the series. Winner takes all in Wellington.

This was the biggest game of Bundee's career. He dearly wanted to show everyone

in New Zealand how good he was. And he
got what he wanted from the start. Ireland
attacked New Zealand from the kick-off and
scored straight from a lineout.

**Ireland are through again! Three
Saturdays in a row. Three early tries.
Josh van der Flier is the man who touches
it down!**

The Irish fans went wild.

'You're the man, Joshy!' roared Bundee, as
he jumped on Josh's back, shaking his fist in
the air.

Soon it got even better. Ireland scored
again. Hugo Keenan grabbed a try and Johnny
Sexton added a penalty.

It wasn't long before a third try came.

**Sheehan ... Sexton ... Bundee
Aki ... Over the line, Robbie
Henshawwwwwww! Ireland are putting
their foot on the throat of the All Blacks!**

'You should have passed it back to me. I
want a try!!!' joked Bundee to Robbie.

'No chance!' replied Robbie, laughing.

It was a classic combination. Ever since their early days playing together at Connacht, Bundee and Robbie Henshaw were like brothers. They spent all their time together. When they played in the centre together, the pair just clicked. Each player always knew exactly what the other was thinking. They barely needed to speak on the pitch.

It was hard to believe. Ireland were 22-3 ahead at half-time. But, just as everyone expected, the All Blacks hit back hard. They scored two quick-fire tries. Suddenly the game was tied.

Bundee could feel the match slipping away. He had completely run out of gas. But every one of the Irish players put their bodies on the line. Eventually, their reward came.

Good surge from Ireland ... Herring ... He stretches and he's got there! Can you believe it?!

Then the referee blew the full-time whistle. They had done it. History. An epic win.

Bundee couldn't believe it. The stadium

erupted with noise. All the Irish players ran onto the pitch and danced in a group hug. Peter O'Mahony broke down in tears. It was an emotional moment for Bundee.

'As a kid I never thought I'd play against and beat the All Blacks,' he said to Robbie on the pitch afterwards. 'Life is strange. But I couldn't be happier!'

'I wouldn't want anyone else by my side for this,' said Robbie. 'Especially as you set up my try for me!'

***

The win in New Zealand was a big statement from the Irish team. It meant they went to the World Cup in France as the number-one ranked side. Like the rest of his teammates, Bundee really wanted to do something special on the biggest stage of all. He felt his teammates were ready to challenge for the title and he worked harder than ever to make sure he played his part. He arrived in France in the shape of his life.

It was clear for everyone to see that
Bundee meant business right from the start.
He scored two tries in the opening game, a
thumping 82-8 win over Romania.

**Bundee Aki ... Presses the accelerator ...
brings the power ... Tryyyyy!**

**Mack Hansen ... To Bundee Aki ...
Straight through and it's try number 11
for Ireland!**

It was a similar story in the next match.
Bundee got two more tries in another easy win.

**Bundee Aki bursting through ...
Bundee bags a tryyyyy!**

**Ireland working hard at the fringes ...
Out the back from Casey ... Bundee Aki ...
He's got another one!**

Bundee was already one of the stars of
the tournament in France. He had shown
his attacking talents. But in the next match,
he needed to be at his defensive best.
Ireland were up against the world champions
South Africa in Paris. Bundee pulled out a
performance for the ages in a thrilling game.

Ireland had to cling on at the end for a dramatic, hard-fought 13-8 win.

It was a night nobody there would ever forget. The party went on long after the final whistle. The Irish fans refused to leave the stadium and had a singsong with the players on the pitch. The players did a lap of honour, as the fans belted out the team's song of the World Cup.

'It's in your head ... In your head ... Zombie ... Zombie ... Zombie!'

'Can you hear that?' said Bundee to Peter O'Mahony as they clapped and cheered the fans. 'Bundee ... Bundee ... Bundee!'

The other players burst out laughing.

'I'm afraid not, Bundee!' said Johnny Sexton with a snigger. 'It's Zombie they're singing. Not Bundee!'

'Well, I choose what I want to hear!' said Bundee. 'And I choose to believe they're singing for me!'

It was a great way to end a perfect night. But sadly, that was the highlight of their

World Cup journey. Bundee scored another memorable try in a game for the ages in Ireland's quarter-final loss to New Zealand. It was his first time scoring against his home country. A special moment. But when the final whistle blew, it meant nothing to him. He had set his heart on winning the World Cup with Ireland. But now the dream had died. A heartbreaking 28-24 defeat had crushed Ireland's World Cup hopes.

Bundee was devastated in the dressing room afterwards. The whole team were. But like Andy and the rest of the team, they vowed to continue. To come back stronger and go for glory once more.

Bundee was nominated as one of the players of the tournament and he finished the season on the shortlist for World Player of the Year. It was a huge personal achievement for someone who thought his rugby dream had ended at the age of 18. He had come a long way from the brave boy in Auckland, who drove his coaches crazy and never did what he was told. He had become a man, moved to the other side of the world and made a new life in Ireland, wearing the green shirt with passion and pride. He had four children now and lived with his wife in Galway. It was more than a home to him. But he didn't want this journey to end in defeat. He still felt he had more in the tank. He promised to bounce back better than ever in next year's Six Nations.

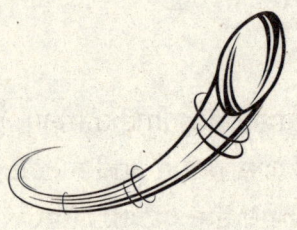

Chapter 12

Slaying the Dragon

Bundee was raring to go for training after he finished his breakfast of champions. He skipped onto the pitch with a spring in his step. It was a Six Nations game week and life was rosy. Ireland had made a fine start with the big win away to France and then the demolition of Italy. Now they were preparing to take on Wales in Dublin. From the outside, everything looked good. But, inside the camp, Andy Farrell was worried.

Slaying the Dragon

Injuries were starting to pile up. Hugo Keenan had hurt his knee in the win over Italy and was ruled out of the Wales game. Garry Ringrose and Mack Hansen were already out of action, so Andy had a few problems to sort out in defence.

He gathered the players into the team room for a chat at the start of the week.

'We've done well, boys,' he said, as the players listened to his every word. 'We're in the hunt but it's all about Wales now. We have to focus on that. We've a few out injured. But that's an opportunity for you guys in here. Now's your chance. Make the most of it. That's what we want. We want you to be tested. We want to see if you can win when the chips are down. So get focused. Get ready. Make this the best training week of your lives.'

Andy was at his best when speaking to the players. He wanted his teams to form a bond both on and off the pitch. He believed that was the best way to success. He loved testing the players and challenging them to see how far they could go.

When it came to naming his team, Andy had one big call to make. Who would replace Hugo Keenan at full-back? Hugo was one of the best in the business and any team in the world would miss him.

But Andy had seen enough in training all week to know who he would pick. Leinster's Ciarán Frawley had all the skills to take Hugo's place. He mostly played at out-half but was equally at home at full-back. Andy always liked him as a player and had no hesitation in calling him up when the time came. After training on Tuesday, he gave him the nod.

'Frawls!' shouted Andy to Ciarán as he walked off the pitch after training. 'You'll be starting at full-back on Saturday. Make sure you've all the work done. I know you can do it. Play your natural game. You're ready.'

Ciarán felt like he was ten feet tall. His heart was pumping with excitement.

'Thanks, Faz,' was all he could say. 'I won't let you down.'

When matchday came, Ciarán Frawley's

family and friends were in their seats early, excited for the biggest day of his career. There were 50,000 others there too in the Aviva Stadium, expecting another Irish victory.

Ciarán was nervous in the dressing room beforehand. But he knew he was in safe hands. He looked at the experience in the team around him. Peter O'Mahony, Tadhg Furlong, Tadhg Beirne, Bundee Aki and Robbie Henshaw. He knew they wouldn't be long telling him if he put a foot wrong.

'Just play your own game and relax,' said captain Peter O'Mahony, as the players walked out of the tunnel and onto the pitch. The crowd roared and Ciarán felt a surge of pride. This was the moment he had dreamed of. A first Six Nations start for Ireland.

He swung his arms around to warm up his shoulders, took a deep breath and clapped his hands. This was it.

The action was thick and fast from the start. Jack Crowley steadied the nerves with an early penalty. And then came the first try.

Ireland with a driving maul ... They have a push on ... Gibson-Park joins in ... Crowley is there too ... Robbie Henshaw adds his muscle ... And they're over the line ... Tryyyyy! Dan Sheehan touches down but the entire Irish team can take credit for that one!

Soon, the Welsh defence cracked again.

Wales are offside ... Here's Crowley ... Nash ... James Lowe ... Tryyyyy! That is one for the mantelpiece!

Ireland were in complete control, leading 17-0 at half-time. But any hope of repeating the Italy scoreline was short-lived. Wales pushed forward early in the second half and Tadhg Beirne found himself in trouble.

Yellow card!

'Off you go for ten minutes in the sin bin,' said the referee, as he awarded Wales a penalty try.

With just over ten minutes to go, the score remained 17-7 to Ireland. It was tighter than they might have hoped. But they kept going looking for a third try. Eventually, they found a way through the stubborn Welsh defence. And it was the player making his first start who got it.

Gibson-Park ... Must be for Frawley ... Ciarán Frawley ... Tryyyyy!

'Yeahhhhhhh!' roared Ciarán as he touched the ball down. His first try for Ireland. He knew his family and friends were right in front of him in the crowd but he couldn't see them as the celebrations were so wild.

'Yes, Frawls!' said Gibson-Park, as they high-fived. 'Some line you ran!'

'Yeah, well, the pass wasn't bad either, Jamo,' replied Ciarán with a smile.

The game was won by now. But Ireland still wanted the bonus point. Wave after wave of green jerseys pushed on in attack.

Doris ... Crowley ... Tadhg Beirne ... Tryyyyy! Tadhg Beirne gets over the line and Ireland get the bonus point win!

It was another perfect day out for Ireland. A 31-7 win over Wales made it three wins from three. They were really motoring now.

Andy Farrell made his way straight to Ciarán Frawley after the final whistle.

'Great game, Frawls!' he said, as he patted him on the back. 'You've worked hard for a long time. You deserve a day like today. Enjoy it!'

Andy always made sure to make every member of the squad feel important. It wasn't just about the star players, or the ones who started every match. He knew success only came when every single player in the squad was happy and they all worked together.

Ciarán was delighted. A win and a try. What more could he ask for on his Six Nations debut?

He made his way over to a special guest in the stands. His grandad was there to watch his star performance. He had supported Ciarán since he was a boy and always encouraged him. He wrapped his arms tightly around him and they shared a strong hug.

'I'm so proud of you,' said his grandad, as tears ran down his face.

'I'll never forget this moment,' replied Ciarán.

Back in the dressing room, Andy had more words of wisdom.

'Three down. Two to go, boys,' he said calmly, as the players relaxed after a hard-fought win. 'The next match is the hardest yet, so enjoy yourselves tonight. But look after yourselves. We've a big week ahead of us.'

He was right. The next match was against England at Twickenham. Never an easy place to go. If Ireland wanted to win a Grand Slam, they would have to do it the hard way. It was win or bust in London.

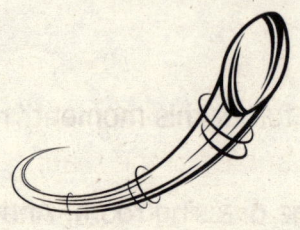

Chapter 13
One Big Family

One of the secrets of Andy Farrell's success
as a coach was the way he brought players
together. He believed a winning team should be
one big family. The players were encouraged
to treat each other like brothers. The coaches
were like parents. There to help and guide the
players along, but also to give out to them if
they stepped out of line.

Andy also welcomed the players' own
families into the fold. Wives, girlfriends

and partners were welcome at matches, celebrations and even the team hotel when they travelled. When new players were presented with their first caps, their parents were brought along to the ceremony. Andy believed that parents played an important role in a player's path to the top. They made a lot of sacrifices along the way. So it was only right that they got to join in on the moments of success too. It was a special part of being involved in this Ireland squad. That's what forged the bond between the players. And that bond was at its strongest when players went through a hard time off the pitch.

The time after the World Cup in France was difficult for Tadhg Furlong. The giant prop from Wexford was one of the most important players in the Irish team. He was as strong as an ox and had serious skills to match. He was one of the best players in the world in his position. He played a vital role in the scrum, where intelligence was needed as much as strength. He loved battling his opponent at scrum-time and he was a fearsome prospect running at defenders when he found himself in space. When he wasn't training on the pitch or pounding weights in the gym, he would usually be on his laptop, watching videos of matches and trying to hone his scrum technique.

Like most of the players in the Ireland squad, Tadhg had great support from his family over the years. His dad James was his number one fan. He was a huge rugby supporter and a big presence at his club, New Ross. He was a butcher, and a great character well-known by everyone in the town. He brought Tadhg and his brother along to training at the club when they were boys, and the rest is history. With the support of his father and his mother Margaret, Tadhg grew up to become one of the world's best rugby players. His dad went to watch all Tadhg's games when he could and was never short of a word of advice after the game.

Tadhg's mam and dad made the trip to France for the World Cup. They were so proud to see their son in action. The epic win over

One Big Family

South Africa was one of the greatest moments of their lives. Afterwards they shared a big hug with Tadhg. It was a moment none of them would ever forget.

Sadly, the World Cup was the last time Tadhg's dad got to see his son play for Ireland. He died later that year, just before Christmas, after a battle with cancer. Tadhg was heartbroken.

It seemed the whole town of New Ross turned out for the funeral. Tadhg and his family were blown away by the support. Of course, his teammates were there to comfort him. That's what it meant to be teammates. They were there for each other on the good days and the bad.

Tadhg took a break from the game for a while to spend more time with his family. But he was back in action in time for the Six Nations. He knew it would be difficult playing on without seeing his dad's familiar face on the sideline. But he was determined to honour him the best way he could. By winning matches out on the pitch.

Coming back to play was hard at first. He couldn't have done it without the support of his teammates. Not least his front row partner and fellow prop, Andrew Porter. He knew exactly what Tadhg was going through. He had lost his mother Wendy to cancer when he was 12. She was the kindest person Andrew had ever known. He was completely devastated when she died. He was just starting secondary school at St Andrew's College in Dublin at the time. He suffered a lot and missed his mam every day.

Rugby became a great release for him. It was the best way he knew to make himself feel better. He always wished she could have seen him as he grew and developed into a star player for Leinster and Ireland. He knew she would have been so proud of him. He has her name tattooed along his left arm, one of the many that cover his body. Even now when Andrew plays, he believes he hears his mother's voice in the crowd, encouraging him.

So Andrew was one of the first players to throw his arms around Tadhg when he joined the Ireland camp for the Six Nations. He didn't have to say much. Tadhg knew that Andrew was there for him. It was exactly what the coach wanted to see from his team. Close on the pitch but even closer off it. Andy wanted his players to be themselves. He liked it when they showed their softer side. He liked it when they made mistakes and admitted it. When they told each other how they were really feeling deep down inside. To Andy that was what being a good teammate meant. It was powerful.

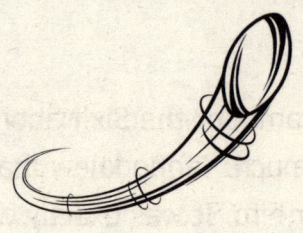

Chapter 14
Twickenham Test

Ireland knew their next match would be
another tough test. They were playing
England away and Twickenham was never an
easy place to go. For years, Twickenham was
a bad place for Irish rugby. Ireland nearly
always lost there. Recently, they had been
more successful. But that didn't make it any
easier.

Ireland travelled to London knowing a
win and a four-try bonus point would secure

the Six Nations Championship. What's more, it would line up a potential shot at a Grand Slam at home to Scotland the following week. Everybody thought Ireland were going to win. They were the reigning Six Nations champions. They had won their first three matches comfortably. England had just lost to Scotland. And Ireland had beaten England four times in their last four matches. Everything was pointing to an Ireland win. But Andy had a bad feeling.

Andy knew just how difficult it was going to be. He was an Englishman after all! England hadn't been the best team in recent years. But they'd had a good World Cup and were building for the future with a new team. He warned everyone in the Irish camp to be wary. Their season was on the line.

There was good news in the build-up to the game. Hugo Keenan had been passed fit to start. He came back into the team in place of Ciarán Frawley. It was tough on Frawley after he'd played so well in the win over Wales. But that's just sport. He knew it better than most. He had to be ready once more to play his role from the substitutes' bench.

London was buzzing on the day of the match. The weather was mild, and the fans were in good spirits. They were mostly dressed in white, cheering for England. But a good crowd of Irish supporters managed to get their hands on tickets. They were easy to spot in their green jerseys, hats and scarves.

In the dressing room before the game, Andy's message was short and to the point.

'This is England. At home. It doesn't matter what's gone before,' he said, as he walked around the room, looking at the players as he moved. 'They will hunt you down. They will put the pressure on. We have to be on our guard. Bring controlled aggression. Trust your skills. Back yourselves.' He finished his short speech with a big clap.

'Let's go, boys!' roared Peter O'Mahony. Ireland were ready for action.

They made a great start. Just three minutes in, Jack Crowley landed the first penalty to put Ireland three points in front.

Great kick! He's really settling into the shirt of Johnny Sexton. It's a snug fit!

But England soon struck back. James Lowe hit a loose clearing kick downfield. It fell to George Furbank. He fed Tommy Freeman, who thundered into Calvin Nash. The Irish winger was floored.

Owwwww!

Nash was down, injured and out of the game. There was a huge gap in the defence now and England found the space. They moved it quickly out wide.

Ollie Lawrence on the wing ... Tryyyyy! England are in front.

'Keep the heads, boys,' shouted Peter O'Mahony. 'It's still early.'

But Ireland's day wasn't getting any better. Calvin Nash was still down. He was injured and in a lot of pain. The doctor came on.

'I'm sorry, Nashy,' he said calmly. 'It was a brave tackle. But your day's over.'

England added another penalty to stretch their lead to 8-3. But Ireland clawed their way back into the game. It wasn't pretty. But Crowley managed to land three more penalties. So, against the run of play, Ireland were 12-8 in front at half-time. It was an exciting game that was right in the balance.

Andy wasn't happy with what he had seen from Ireland. But he kept things positive in the dressing room.

'You've hardly played at all this half, boys, but you're still in front. That's a great sign,' he said. 'Let's pick up the tempo. Up the aggression. This match is here to be won!'

Feeling energised, the players prepared to go back out for the biggest half of rugby in their season. Their Grand Slam dream was in sight. But only just.

Andy's words were still ringing in their ears when they crashed over the try line.

There's space outside for Ireland ...

Henshaw ... Gets it wide to Lowe ... James Looooowwwwwwwwe! The flying winger is on the end of it again!

It was a flying acrobatic finish. The crowd gasped in admiration. The Irish fans went wild.

'Yes, Lowey!' screamed Robbie Henshaw, as he jumped on top of him.

It looked like Ireland were getting on top in the game. But suddenly, England hit back once more. Again, it was another run from deep that caused Ireland problems.

Underhill ... To Itoje ... And it's George Furbank ...

Tryyyyy!

What a game! You can't take your eyes off it!

The Irish players were disgusted. They knew they shouldn't have let England score from that far out. Peter O'Mahony called them in for a huddle.

'No more stupid mistakes,' he roared. 'We're still 17-13 in front. Don't panic. Don't throw this away!'

But it was the captain himself who was in trouble a few minutes later. England were on the attack and Peter O'Mahony jumped on the ball to stop them. The referee wasn't happy. He blew his whistle sharply. It was a penalty for England. Peter knew he was wrong.

'Sorry, sir,' he pleaded with the referee. But it was no good.

A yellow card!

He was sent to the sin bin for ten minutes.

England took quick advantage of the extra man. They threw everything at Ireland, attacking the line again and again. Ireland's defence held firm for as long as they could. But eventually they cracked.

Ben Earl ... He's popping up everywhere ... And the powerhouse powers over ... Tryyyyy! England are in front.

England led 20-17 with ten minutes to go. Ireland were under pressure. Their Grand Slam dreams were about to go up in smoke. But they kept their cool and trusted the process.

Conor Murray was ordering the players about from scrum-half as they attacked inside England's 22. Eventually there was a bit of space, and he sent the ball wide.

Murray ... Finds Crowley ... To Henshaw ... To Gibson-Park and Loooooooooowe ... Tryyyyy! James Lowe with another one ... Is that the try that wins the game for Ireland?

The crowd gasped as Jack Crowley missed a tricky conversion. With the clock ticking down, Ireland led by just two points. It was agonising. England had the ball and were on the attack. The Irish players tackled themselves to a standstill. They were brave and fearless as they tried to keep England out. But the home side kept coming. Their will to win was strong too. The fans roared them on. The Irish fans screamed back. The noise was deafening. The pressure was intense. Then came a moment that nobody expected.

The clock is into the red ... England need a miracle. They fancy a drop goal ...

They're going for it ... It comes out to Marcus Smith ... He swings his boot ... And it's over! England have won it with the last kick of the game!

Marcus Smith's drop goal landed the three points England needed to snatch victory. The Irish players fell to the ground. They had lost by 23 points to 22. The narrowest defeat imaginable. It was the cruellest way to lose. Their Grand Slam dreams were over.

The English players celebrated wildly, jumping up and down and dancing. Ireland's players could only watch them in disbelief. Seconds ago, they were on for a Grand Slam. Now they were gone. It was hard to take.

The players said nothing. You could hear a pin drop in the dressing room. Andy said a few words.

'Chin up, boys!' he said, as the players held their heads in their hands. 'You gave it your all. It wasn't to be. That's sport. But there's still something to fight for next week. We can still win the Six Nations. Let's remember this feeling. Take it all in and tell yourself you're never going to feel this way again. You learn more from defeat than victory. Learn the lessons and we move on. It's Scotland next week at home, with a championship on the line. That's a huge prize. So let's go for it!'

It was a gut-wrenching defeat for the Irish team. The players were heartbroken. But, as ever, Andy had picked up their spirits. He was right. There was still a championship to play for. And they would need to be at their best to beat Scotland in Dublin the following weekend.

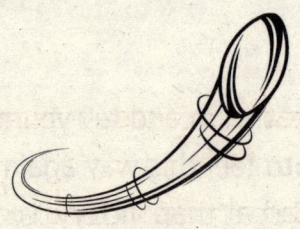

Chapter 15
JGP

The defeat to England stung for several reasons. Ireland felt they had done enough to win the game but left some big chances behind them. Luck just hadn't been with them. The early injury to Calvin Nash had disrupted the whole team. The enforced changes meant scrum-half Jamison Gibson-Park played most of the match on the wing. It was just one of those days when anything that could go wrong did go wrong.

Gibson-Park had become a driving force of

the Ireland team over recent seasons. He was a nippy number 9. A pacy player with a pass to match. He had a great rugby brain and could see things before others. He was a fine kicker too. But his commitment was what marked him out from the others. It takes a special player to move out of position for the good of the team and still put in a standout performance. JGP, as he was known, was one of those who put the team ahead of himself. And his teammates felt lucky to have him.

Like James Lowe and Bundee Aki, JGP came to Ireland the long way. He too grew up in New Zealand, in a remote place called Great Barrier Island. It was a perfect home for a child to grow up in. Only 800 people lived on the island, so everyone knew each other. It was a friendly community and Jamison loved it. Life was lived outdoors in the countryside. He spent most of his time surfing, fishing and diving. The sea was always a big part of his life. His dad was a keen diver, so Jamison and his brothers joined him when they could.

Ireland's Call

Jamison loved sport. He spent most of his time with a ball in his hands. As soon as school finished, he would head to the pitch for a game of rugby. The only rule he had was to be home before dark.

When he got older, his family moved to the mainland and Jamison began a new life at Gisborne Boys' High School. The teachers there spotted his sporting talent straight away. He was a great athlete, fast and skilful. But he was considered small for a rugby player. Many people told him he would never make it to the top.

When he was a teenager, he decided to give up the game for a while. He let the negative comments get to him. He believed he was too small to become a professional rugby player. He stopped trying. He switched his attention to other sports for a while. Living so close to the sea, he loved surfing. He dreamed of being a professional surfer one day. But as time passed, he missed playing rugby with his teammates. He decided to go back and give it another go. It turned out to be the right choice.

Jamison became a standout player for his school, which meant he was picked for the New Zealand schools' team. That led to an offer from his regional team Taranaki. And after catching the eye playing for them, he moved up to Super Rugby to play for the Blues, one of the biggest clubs in New Zealand. In a few short years, he had climbed his way to the top of the club game in his home country.

But Jamison's time in Super Rugby was a little difficult. He was often on the subs bench, and he found it hard to break into the starting team. He was a long way off a call-up for the All Blacks. He worked hard and did what he could. But his path to the national team was blocked by a group of super-talented players. He felt it might be time for a new challenge.

He didn't think twice when the offer to move to Leinster came through. Just like Bundee Aki and James Lowe, JGP was soon packing his bags for Ireland. It was a huge change, but he couldn't wait to get stuck in.

He wasn't an instant hit at Leinster. He

was star-struck by Johnny Sexton and his teammates at his first training session. He couldn't believe he was on the other side of the world, training with some of the big hitters of the global game. He had to pinch himself sometimes.

But as time passed, he began to find his feet. He was eventually called up to the starting team and made an instant impression.

Gibson-Park ... On his first start ... Scores a tryyyyy for Leinster!

From then on, he never looked back.

Jamison became a vital member of a successful Leinster team. Three years later, when he was allowed to play for Ireland, he grabbed the chance with both hands.

When Andy took over the Ireland team from Joe Schmidt, he wanted to do some things differently. One was to get the team to play quicker. He wanted his scrum-half to speed the game up. To take the ball on themselves and run at the opposition. To drive the team forward. In JGP, he had found the perfect player.

'Just play your own game,' said Andy to Jamison in the tunnel before his first match for Ireland. They were playing Italy at the Aviva Stadium.

'I just use my eyes and ears and follow the game,' said Jamison, giving a cheeky grin. Andy had never seen a player so relaxed.

Jamison impressed Andy with his performance that day. Before long, he was one of the first names on the team sheet.

JGP played a vital role in Ireland's success under Andy Farrell. But now Andy wanted more. Once Johnny Sexton retired after the World Cup, Jamison knew he was going to have to step up. Ireland needed a new leader to drive the team forward from behind the scrum. JGP was just the man. He rose to the challenge and played out some superb man-of-the-match performances. He wasn't one for shouting and screaming on the pitch. He liked to let his play do the talking. But he became a quietly inspirational force for Ireland. His enforced move to play on the wing at

Twickenham had impressed everyone. He was the best player on the pitch, even though he played out of position.

Jamison realised how upset his teammates were at the final whistle. But as one of the older, more experienced players now, he knew he had to keep their heads in the game. Growing up on an island made him a relaxed, calm guy. He needed all of that now.

'Losing hurts. We're all upset. But we can't sit here and feel sorry for ourselves,' he said, as he tried to lift his teammates' spirits. 'There are plenty of teams who'd swap places with us,' he continued. 'We still have a championship to win. Let's make sure we go out there against Scotland next week and give a performance we can be proud of.'

Ireland, and JGP, were ready to bounce back.

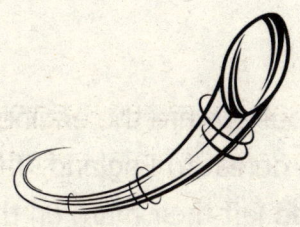

Chapter 16

Bouncing Back

The players didn't have time to feel sorry for themselves after the loss to England. It was a tight turnaround to their final game against Scotland. Back at the training camp on Monday morning, they were keen to put defeat behind them and focus on the task at hand. There was a championship to be won, after all.

Second-row Tadhg Beirne was one of the first into camp. He met Josh van der Flier and Caelan Doris on the way to training. These three powerhouses were the engine of the Irish team. Even in defeat to England, Tadhg, Josh and Caelan had left their mark on the pitch. They always gave one hundred per cent.

Tadhg was a tall, athletic player who had grown up in County Kildare. He went to school in Clongowes Wood, the same place as Dan Sheehan. He was a great schools' player and joined the Leinster Academy when he finished. But things didn't work out exactly how he wanted. He struggled to get into the senior team.

After a few years of frustration he took the brave step of moving to Wales to play for the Scarlets. It was a great move. He got the chance to show everyone what he could do. He became one of the best players in the league within a few short years. Then he returned to Ireland, this time with Munster, where he became a star.

Equally at home in the back row or the second row, his specialty was disrupting other teams at the breakdown. He was one of the best defensive players in the world.

Bouncing Back

'Big week for you, Tadhg!' said Josh, as they began to change for training.

'Sure is, Josh. Fifty caps. It's hard to believe,' said Tadhg as he took off his runners and pulled his boots from his bag.

Tadhg and Josh were great friends off the pitch. They had both come so far together. Josh had gone from playing as a schoolboy in Wicklow, to Leinster, Ireland and all the way to being crowned World Player of the Year. Now his friend Tadhg was set to play his 50th match in green.

'There was a time I thought I'd never even play once for Ireland,' said Tadhg. 'It's hard to believe this is going to be my 50th time.'

'Well, let's make sure we make it a day to remember,' said Caelan Doris, joining in the conversation.

Caelan was a colossus at number 8 for Ireland and Leinster. He had grown up a long way from the rugby heartlands of Ireland, in a place called Lacken outside Ballina in Mayo. He'd gone to a tiny school, where he was the only boy in his class. He took his first steps on the rugby pitch with the club in Ballina. Everyone there knew he was a huge talent straight away. He moved to Dublin to go to secondary school at Blackrock College, where he became a hero on the rugby pitch. They had a star-studded team with future rugby stars like Nick Timoney, Joey Carbery, Conor Oliver and Jeremy Loughman, and together they won the Leinster Schools Senior Cup.

Caelan was the one who stood out more than most. He had it all. It didn't surprise anyone when he was fast-tracked all the way to the senior national team. He was right at home from his first match and now many thought he could be a future captain.

'I'm glad we've a big game this week,' he said to Josh and Tadhg as he pulled his training top over his head. 'Gets the England game out of the system.'

'Yeah, the less said about England the better,' said Josh. He hated losing.

'It's gonna be some atmosphere on Saturday,' said Tadhg, trying to keep things positive. 'I can't wait to get out there. You don't get a chance to win a Six Nations Championship every day!'

The three finished getting changed, grabbed their energy drinks and snacks and headed for the training pitch. It was time to get serious again. Scotland were coming to town for a Six Nations decider and Ireland had work to do.

Peeeep!

Andy Farrell blew his whistle.

'Gather in, boys!' he roared, as coaches Paul O'Connell and Simon Easterby stood beside him in the centre of the pitch.

'England is over,' he barked. 'That's the last time we'll mention it. It's all about Saturday now. There's a Six Nations Championship to be won. It's a huge opportunity for each and every one of you. Beat Scotland and you'll be the champions. In front of your home crowd. Your family and friends watching on. It's everything. Don't waste the chance. The hard work starts today.'

Josh could feel his legs twitching. He was ready to go once more.

Tadhg took a moment to think of his journey to this point. He wanted his 50th cap to be a special occasion. 'I need to win this,' he thought to himself.

Caelan listened to Andy's every word. He loved his speeches. Andy always seemed to know exactly what to say.

Caelan looked around at his teammates gathered in a huddle. Hugo Keenan, Calvin Nash, James Lowe, Robbie Henshaw, Bundee Aki, Jack Crowley, Jamison Gibson-Park, Andrew Porter, Dan Sheehan, Tadhg Furlong, Joe McCarthy, Tadhg Beirne, Peter O'Mahony and Josh van der Flier. The substitutes, coaches and support staff. They were all in this together. Each of them was determined to put the England defeat behind them. Each one was ready to do what was needed to beat Scotland and win the Six Nations.

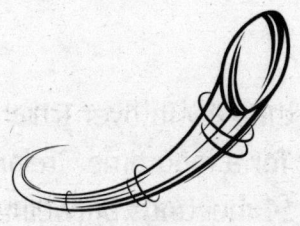

Chapter 17
The Decider

That Saturday, everything was on the line. It was St Patrick's weekend. Dublin was buzzing and everybody was hoping Ireland would win the match. Everyone except Scotland. They had come to spoil the party.

The Scots were having a good Six Nations themselves. They'd beaten England and Wales and were looking to add Ireland to the list to win the Triple Crown. There was a bit of bad blood between the teams too. Scotland loved nothing more than a win over Ireland. But they hadn't done it for a long time. Ireland had won 13 of the last 14 meetings between the teams.

Andy Farrell was able to name an unchanged team for the game. Calvin Nash had recovered from the head injury he'd suffered against England. Andy decided to give the team that lost in Twickenham another go. But just before kick-off there was a change of plan.

Owwwww!

Hugo Keenan pulled up injured during the warm-up. He was out of the match. Jordan Larmour was called in as his replacement. It was a big disruption to the team. But Andy was confident Jordan was ready to play. It was what he had planned for. He wanted his team to be able to adapt to bad situations. This was just another example.

Before kick-off, the players went through their final preparations in the dressing room. Captain Peter O'Mahony gave one last short speech.

'This is what all the work is for. We've done our prep. We know our detail. Just go out and give it your all. Your family and friends are watching. Do it for them. Do it for the jersey. Leave everything out there!' he roared, as the rest of the players clapped and cheered.

Tadhg Beirne led the team onto the pitch to honour his 50th cap. It was a huge moment for him. The anthems played. 'Flower of Scotland' first. Then 'Amhrán na bhFiann', followed by 'Ireland's Call'. The stadium was shaking by the end of it.

Peter O'Mahony was overcome by emotion. A tear trickled down his cheek as he squeezed his eyes firmly shut. The fans were hoping to see history. The players could feel the pressure. A light drizzle began to fall as Scotland's number 10, Finn Russell, took the ball in hand to start the game.

Here. We. Go!

It was Scotland who settled first. Russell had the first kick of the game and sent it straight between the posts. 3-0 to Scotland.

But Ireland quickly struck back with one of the easiest tries of all time. Scotland had a lineout deep inside their own territory. But it all went badly wrong. The hooker threw it way too far. Dan Sheehan was the happiest man in the stadium as he gratefully caught the ball and strolled over the line for the handiest of scores.

Tryyyyy! Scotland have overthrown the lineout right into the hands of Dan Sheehan. And he happily accepts the gift!

'Yes, Dano!' roared Andrew Porter as he joined the celebrations.

'Easy peasy!' said Jamison Gibson-Park, laughing.

Dan just waved his fist in the air in celebration. Ireland were back in the match.

Jack Crowley added the conversion to send Ireland 7-3 clear.

Up in the coaches' box, Andy Farrell slammed the table in delight.

But Ireland's discipline let them down again. They gave away another cheap penalty and Russell slotted it over. 7-6 now and Ireland were getting nervy.

Andy laid down the law at half-time.

'We need to up it,' he roared at the players. 'If you play like that again, you won't be celebrating tonight. Don't let the nerves take you over. Embrace the opportunity. Play your natural game.'

He was right. The players had been unusually tense. But they still had the second half to put things right.

Crowley added a penalty to steady the nerves. Then Tadhg Furlong thought he'd scored a crucial try. The big Wexford prop used all his power to pummel the Scottish defence and touch down over the line. But the referee wasn't sure. He went to the video referee to check.

No try!

There was a huge groan from the crowd. Tadhg had slightly knocked the ball on before he touched it down.

'Unlucky, Tadhg!' said Caelan Doris, as he patted him on the back.

'Keep going, boys!' yelled Peter O'Mahony.

Ireland were knocking on the door now. They were getting closer with every play. The

Scottish players were tiring. Garry Ringrose made a stunning break. Then Robbie Henshaw thought he was over the line, but the Scots held on again. Time was ticking down. The Six Nations was at stake. Ireland were running out of ideas. But, as ever, they kept going. They didn't know any other way.

It's Kelleher ... Beirne ... Ireland ... Against a Scottish defence that refuses to wilt ...

Tryyyyy! Andrew Porter finds the answer. He unlocks the Scottish defence!

Andrew roared with delight and threw his arms in the air. He had blood streaming from a cut above his eye, but he didn't care. He looked at the tattoo of his mother's name on his arm and kissed it. He knew she was with him, looking down. He felt she had helped him over the line.

'Yes, Ports!' roared Tadhg Beirne into his ear. Every one of the Irish players were pumped up.

Ireland were 17-6 up with ten minutes to play. They were surely out of sight now.

But they still hadn't done the job. Ireland seemed to fall asleep. And Scotland snuck over the line for a late try.

Away and gone! Huw Jones ... Under the posts. There's stunned silence in the Aviva Stadium!

The Irish players couldn't believe it. He just seemed to slip through. Robbie Henshaw stood with his hands on his head. Ireland's lead was cut to 17-13 with two minutes left to play.

There was still time for Scotland to win it.

There was still time for Ireland's day to turn to disaster.

'Come on, boys!' roared Josh. 'Last push!'

They launched the ball back downfield and defended with their lives. The two minutes seemed to go on forever. But eventually the final whistle sounded.

The game was over. Ireland had held on for a 17-13 victory.

Ireland are the back-to-back Six Nations champions!

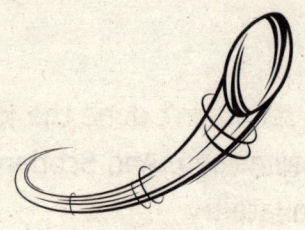

Chapter 18

Team of Us

The celebrations went on long after the final whistle. Ireland were the Six Nations Champions. After everything they had been through, this victory seemed sweeter than most.

The fans went wild in celebration. Andy Farrell punched the air in delight. Peter O'Mahony almost collapsed with exhaustion. James Lowe threw his arms high into the sky and let out a roar that could almost be heard in New Zealand. The team's anthem, 'Zombie', rang out around the stadium.

'They're playing your song!' joked Robbie Henshaw to Bundee Aki, as the pair hugged each other.

Peter O'Mahony took a microphone and spoke to the crowd.

'This is a special group of people. The World Cup really bonded us. It's a huge honour to captain your country and this was a great win.'

He had done it. The young man from Cork Con had risen to the top of the game. It was the greatest honour of his glittering career. The crowd cheered. They hoped it wasn't the last time they would see Peter O'Mahony wearing the green shirt. But if it was, what a way to finish.

Peter made his way over to Jack Crowley. The young out-half was beaming from ear to ear. 'Well done, kid!' he said quietly, as he gave Jack a huge hug. 'First Six Nations and you played like that. You didn't miss a beat!'

Jack was delighted. The boy from Bandon

had stepped into the biggest shoes in Irish rugby and come away smiling. Johnny Sexton was a legend of Irish rugby. But now there was a new hero. In Jack Crowley, the number 10 shirt looked to be in safe hands for years to come.

Jack grabbed his Munster teammate Calvin Nash and took a selfie. It was hard to believe the pair of them had won the title in just their first season in the team.

Big Joe McCarthy was still catching his breath when he joined a group hug with Josh van der Flier, Caelan Doris, Jack Conan and Tadhg Beirne. They were the man mountains of this Irish team. A mix of youth and experience that powered Ireland to victory when it mattered. Joe spotted his family in the crowd and sprinted over to them to celebrate. He shared a special hug with his brothers, Andrew and Paddy. They meant everything to him.

Fireworks crackled into the sky and the fans broke into a rousing rendition of the 'Fields of Athenry'. It was a special moment.

Jamison Gibson-Park was announced as the man of the match. A fitting reward for a player who had reached a new level in this tournament. He stepped back to look at the celebrations. To take it all in. He had to pinch himself. The little boy from a remote island in New Zealand had just become a Six Nations champion. He was so grateful for everything Ireland had given him.

His wife Patti joined him on the pitch, with their daughters Iris and Isabella and their son Jai. James Lowe ran over to them with his baby son Nico. Then Bundee Aki joined them with his family too. They all stood in for a photo. Three boys who had travelled to the other side of the world and given their all in the green jersey of Ireland, now celebrating Six Nations success.

Dan Sheehan found his family too. It seemed like yesterday they had been flying out to Romania for a new adventure together, leaving rugby behind. Now they gathered again in the Aviva Stadium, celebrating his title triumph. Dan had scored five tries in the tournament.

'Not bad for a hooker!' he joked to his brother Bobby.

Robbie Henshaw, Garry Ringrose, Jordan Larmour and a host of other players were getting the party started. Sticking on Ireland hats and scarves and busting out their dance moves.

In a quiet moment, Andrew Porter and Tadhg Furlong shared a hug. The two powerhouse props took time to remember those they had lost. Andrew felt his mother with him. Tadhg wished his dad could have been there.

In the centre of the pitch, Andy Farrell joined the madness. He took special pride in this victory. After the World Cup disappointment in Paris, he had wondered if he could go on. Now he had his answer. The team had survived the loss of Johnny Sexton, their leader and captain, and winger Keith Earls. They had shaken off an injury crisis, disruption

and a defeat to England. They had brought
through a new crop of young Irish stars.

For Andy, this victory was the sweetest of
all.

He gave Peter O'Mahony a huge hug and
whispered in his ear. 'Stay on for another
season,' he said. 'You don't want to leave all
this behind.'

Peter laughed and said nothing. He knew
Andy was right.

Peter stepped up to the podium where the
trophy would be presented. The silver cup
stood glistening in the floodlights with green
ribbons tied to either side. Peter asked Tadhg
Furlong to join him to lift the trophy together. A
special gesture from a special team.

Ohhhhhhhhhh!

The players gathered behind, giddy with
excitement as they waited for their captain to
raise the trophy aloft.

Peter O'Mahony took one side of the trophy
and Tadhg Furlong took the other. The pair
raised the Six Nations Cup high into the air,

as a huge roar erupted across Dublin and
around Ireland. Fireworks sparkled and music
blasted. Andy watched with pride etched on his
face. They had done it. Together. Ireland. The
Six Nations champions. They had answered
Ireland's call.